CW00954181

£1-99

In the Therapist's Mirror

In the Therapist's Mirror

Reality in the Making

Marilyn Wedge

W. W. Norton & Company • New York • London

For information about permission to reproduce selections
from this book, write to
Permissions, W.W. Norton & Company, Inc., 500 Fifth Avenue,
New York, NY 10110

Library of Congress Cataloging-in-Publication Data
Wedge, Marilyn.
    In the therapist's mirror : reality in the making / Marilyn Wedge.
        p.   cm.
    "A Norton professional book."
    Includes bibliographical references and index.
    ISBN 0-393-70235-9
    1. Psychoanalysis—Semiotics.   2. Personal construct therapy.
3. Constructivism (Psychology) . 4. Familiy psychotherapy—Case
studies.   I.   Title.
RC489.S435W43   1996
616.89'14—dc20   96-8687 CIP

W.W. Norton & Company, Inc., 500 Fifth Avenue, New York, NY 10110
http://www.wwnorton.com
W.W. Norton & Company Ltd., 10 Coptic Street, London WC1A 1PU

1 2 3 4 5 6 7 8 9 0

For David Eugene

Contents

Preface and Acknowledgments

THIS BOOK ARISES from my years of practice of strategic family therapy. I came to use the strategic approach because I found that it provided the most effective means of encouraging therapeutic change in the families who consulted me. This book is in some ways a departure from, or—as I would prefer to see it—an extension of strategic therapy. In the practice of therapy, as in other endeavors, experience has been my guide. My experience as a therapist these fourteen years has shown me the importance of symbolic forms in setting the courses of our lives. Myth, for example, is no newcomer to the field of therapy, for Freud built much of his theory upon myth. But the roles of such symbolic forms as myth, ritual, and polysemic language in constructing meaning in therapy need to be reinterpreted in the light of the postmodern era.

Chapter 1 of this book was originally intended to be an Introduction. It sketches the evolution of my thinking about the ways that we construct meaning—in therapy as well as in the rest of experience—in the postmodern world. Chapters 2 through 5 are for the most part theoretical and philosophical explorations of this theme. Chapters 6 through 9 contain detailed case examples of therapies which illustrate the roles of symbolic forms.

I was the therapist in the all of the case examples presented and therefore I have simply used the gender pronoun "she" throughout the book when referring to the therapist.

Chapter 6 originally appeared in somewhat different form in *Case Studies in Brief and Family Therapy*, *8* (1), 1994. I am grateful for permission to reprint it here.

This book could not have been written without the loving support of my family, past and present. I am above all grateful to my parents, Edward and Faye Weltz. My husband Gene has been an abiding source of encouragment and inspiration while I was writing the book, reading, criticizing, disputing, challenging, and occasionally praising every draft of every chapter. Many of the ideas in the book grew out of our dialogues. My daughter, Jessica, and my sons, Daniel and Edward, were ever encouraging, understanding, and supportive of my work.

Friends and colleagues through the years have helped me in various ways. My thanks go to Mary Kastner, M.S., and Suzanne Dudeck, Ph.D. I wish to express my appreciation especially to Margo Estrin, M.D. I am grateful also to Stephen Toulmin for our many conversations on philosophy and ethics. My clients have taught me much and to them I express heartfelt gratitude.

I would like to express special gratitude to Susan Barrows Munro, my editor at Norton, for her sensitive, provocative, and insightful comments on the text, and her enthusiastic support of the book from start to finish. I would also like to thank Regina Ardini at Norton for her work in editing the manuscript. Finally, I am grateful to Jay Haley for reading the final manuscript.

Marilyn Wedge

Norwell, Massachusetts
March, 1996

In the Therapist's Mirror

CHAPTER 1

A Reflected Reality

But at that angle by virtue of the mirror . . . I could see . . . that vast sunset covering the whole sky.

— Milton Erickson

FAMILY THERAPY HAS interdisciplinary origins in anthropology (Bateson), philosophy (Russell and Whitehead), communications theory (Bateson and Jackson), systems theory and cybernetics (von Foerster and von Glasersfeld), and hypnosis (Milton Erickson). Recently, family therapists have continued the field's interdisciplinary tradition by turning to philosophy and to literature for forms of narrative and for the metaphorical and polysemic language of poetry. Along with bringing the forms and structures of narrative into their work, some family therapists have turned also to anthropology, especially to the ideas of Victor Turner and Arnold van Gennep, for the structure and processes of rituals and for the polysemic nature of symbols. What van Gennep called a "rite of passage," with its phases of separation, margin (or *limen*) and aggregation, has provided a useful metaphor for the various transitional processes of social life facilitated by family therapy. Family therapists are also beginning to reflect on culture and the creation

1

of meaning in human experience as inseparable from culture. Salvador Minuchin (1993) has summed up the double confluence of postmodern family therapy with narrative and anthropology:

> [T]herapists are always storytellers. We are like anthropologists, exploring other people's lives. And, like anthropologists, we are inevitably guided by our own experiences in describing others. (p.5)

A therapist's theory and practice of therapy is, as Minuchin tells us, shaped by his or her own experience and culture. The view of "cultural constructivism" I present in this book took shape in the interdisciplinary and constructivist milieu of the University of Chicago, where I was a graduate student in the 1970s. There, as a student in the Committee on Social Thought, I became accustomed to the blurring of boundaries between the traditional fields and disciplines. Students in the Committee were expected to construct their own "fields" of study from a vast diversity of texts, ranging from pre-Socratic philosophy to contemporary literature. Victor Turner's Thursday evening seminars on "comparative symbology" were a *liminal* sea of interdisciplinary creativity, where papers on anthropology mingled with papers on psychology, literature, linguistics, philosophy, religion, and art.

From Turner's seminars emerged unique constructions of group experience and social life, as well as a vivid sense of culture in process. New meanings and forms derived from the myths, rituals, symbols, narratives, and art forms of primitive peoples came to replace empirical and structural concepts that no longer seemed to fit what Turner called the "processual" flow of lived experience. These new meanings gained currency and legitimacy by being performed in the seminars. The reality that was constructed in the seminars was permeated by *cultural* as opposed to *structural* forms. Where the bloodless language of the academic social sciences fell short in describing the vitality of lived experience, new words and new concepts were invented, ever narrowing the gap between expression and experience. Van Gennep's term *liminality* was especially seminal in this regard. The mood of Turner's seminars was subjunctive and hypothetical, typical of the *liminal* stage of initiates, betwixt and between the more structured phases of academic life. Also liminal was the absence of clearly defined hierarchical boundaries. Among the seminar participants, there was an easy familiarity, a mutual outspokenness, the absence of rigid social roles and hierarchies. The experience of connectedness among liminal beings, which Turner called *communitas*, was generated and performed, as students and faculty ate, drank, and engaged in conversation with one another.

THE MULTIVOCALITY OF EXPERIENCE

In 1976, many of the ideas generated in Turner's seminars were brought together at a symposium at the Annual Meetings of the American Anthropological Association in Washington, D.C. The symposium was entitled *Rituals and Myths of Self: Uses of and Occasions for Reflexivity*, and was chaired by Barbara Meyerhoff. Turner and Meyerhoff invited me to present a paper on the myth of Narcissus, which they thought was the central myth of reflexivity, at the symposium. In my paper I argued that this myth was generated by poetic language, language used not referentially or mimetically but *self-referentially* and *reflexively*. Moreover, the myth of Narcissus, which Turner believed was "a profoundly social myth," could be read as a reflexive commentary on this very process. The papers which we presented at the Symposium were later published in a special issue of the journal *Semiotica* under the title *Signs about Signs: the Semiotics of Self-Reference*, edited by Barbara Babcock (1980a).

This symposium on reflexivity influenced my thinking about the implications of language as a system of signs for the world of lived experience. Multivocality, or polysemy, as Turner had always maintained, was a quality not only of poetic language, but of the whole scope of lived, experienced human reality, which could also be read as a construction of signs. As Geertz (1986) put it, in his comments in *The Anthropology of Experience*,

> the passage from what is done to what is meant . . . involves above all a capacity to transcend our deep-grained

assumption that signs are one thing and experience another. (p.380)

Culture, as a semiotic construct, thus closes the gap between language and experience. All collective or cultural experience is *semiosis*, and all cultural experience is, at least in part, reflexive.

REFLEXIVITY

Reflecting upon the system of signs that shapes, molds, and ultimately *creates* our experience leads us to yet another experience, the experience of reflexivity. To reflexively comment upon the system of signs that is cultural experience is, as Babcock points out in her introductory essay to the *Semiotica* papers, to see the limits and boundaries of cultural experience from another standpoint. This point of view is outside or *meta* the very frame of culture upon which we are reflecting. The reflexive use of signs to comment upon signs leads us, if not to a transcendence of signs, at least to novel (and paradoxical) constructions. Thus, cultural performances of all sorts, including myths, are instances of reflexivity. *Mythos* was the Greek word for story. What this suggests is that any account of experience as patterned or framed in stories must concern itself with reflexivity. We may shape our experience and our actions as stories or, to use the ancient word, as myths, but the reverse is true as well.

Babcock (1980a) tells us that reflexivity is a source of novelty that remarks upon various closed systems or, as I would put it, the systems of reality constructed by culture. Reflexivity, writes Babcock,

> reminds us that we have no absolute distinctions between what is "real" and what is "fictional" . . . and that these domains are separated only by a transposition in our modes of attending to what there is. (p.5)

As it seeks a deeper understanding of culture by engaging in reflexivity, which includes the self examination of its own processes, family therapy, like anthropology, is led to re-evaluate the frames, as Bateson called them, which various cultures place upon experience. Ultimately, we arrive at the paradoxical question of whether our real life experience is framed as stories, or whether the real stories, the myths, frame us.

RITUAL AND DRAMA

The unique structures of collective experience which Turner and other anthropologists of experience have brought to light are now being explored by many family therapists, with their interest in analogical language, story telling, polysemy, paradox, trance states, spirituality, rites of repentance and reparation, ordeals, rites of passage or transition, and reflexivity. Literary and aesthetic forms have seized the day in family therapy, whether in the re-storying of life experience by narrative means, or in the strategic use of paradoxical pretends to perform new family dramas, or in the use of stories to induce trance states, or in the constructing of metaphorical and reciprocal sequences in families. Reflection on the variety of practical ways to bring about change in people's lives has generated a number of theories. Theories, or at least theories that are useful, spring, as the pragmatist philosopher John Dewey pointed out, from a context of problem-solving inquiry. And in the emerging theories we find that family therapy is expanding from a technique for changing a person's life to a philosophical account of how we know, or how we construct, reality through the mirrors of analogical language and aesthetic forms. Experience in the therapy room has disclosed new and unique patterns of group experience, unlocked by multivocal or polysemic language, and the multivocal symbols of rituals. The appeal of theories that spring from the practice of therapy is that they are grounded in the activity of solving family problems in practice. For the practitioner of good conscience is faced on a daily basis with the unrelenting questions: "Does my theory of human behavior and motivation work in practice to bring about change in people's lives? Does my theory, in fact, relieve human suffering and misery?"

It seems likely, as Turner suggests, that poetic language and literary forms fit group experience precisely because they originated in group experience. Turner was influenced by Dewey's idea that the forms organizing the flux of *lived* experience were *aesthetic* not *conceptual* forms. And, according to Turner, aesthetic forms, particularly those of the dramatic arts, are rooted in what he called rituals of redress. This view was espoused earlier by the cultural historian Johan Huizinga. Huizinga (1950) argued, in a vein similar to Turner's, that both drama and poetry sprang from sacred rituals. Of Greek tragedy, Huizinga writes, "Far from being literature designed for the stage it was originally a sacred play or a played rite" (p. 144). And Turner (1986) tells us in one of his last papers, "The point I would make here is that the world of theater . . . and the immense variety of theatrical subgenres, derive . . . from redress as ritual process" (p.47). Here we find a link between therapy and aesthetic form, since redressive rituals delve into the hidden causes of misfortune and attempt to cure them by analogical or symbolic means — not unlike the processes of therapy. The narrative therapist David Epston makes explicit the connection between therapy and redressive rituals when he "diagnoses" curses and maledictions in the context of family therapy (White & Epston, 1990).

ANALOGICAL COMMUNICATION

"We live in analogies and metaphors," mused Jay Haley at the 1993 Washington, D.C. conference on *Integration*. And, according to Michael White (1990), the "analogies" we choose are what we use to pull out order and meaning from an inchoate world. Family therapy has been from its beginnings a theory of analogical communication. In the early years of family therapy, analogical communication was understood as the sending and receiving of messages with multiple referents, particularly in the context of significant relationships. Analogical communication, as opposed to digital communication, was observed to be essentially ambiguous and dependent on context for meaning (Jackson, 1968).

Even more relevant to our discussion here was the observation that an analogical communication not only has multiple referents, but is also an *instance* of its referent, with the important implication that the problems of logical typing are quite different for analogical than for digital communication (Bateson, Jackson, Haley & Weakland, in Jackson, 1968). In the context of analogical communication, which is the context not only of poetry but also, as Bateson's research showed, of human behavior, sign and thing are no longer necessarily distinct logical types. Bateson pointed out that a sign can both signify a behavior and be an instance of that behavior. Signs and things are continuous, tangled, or folded in upon one another. Analogical language, in a creative twist, turns back on itself and creates an analogical model of human reality.

FAMILY THERAPY AND PHILOSOPHY

Thus, in the postmodern era, the scope and meaning of analogical communication have broadened beyond the transmitting and receiving of messages in relationships. Analogical communication has become the way we construct reality itself, or at least the way we construct a reality that has some sort of experienced or practical meaning for us. With constructivism and the inquiry into analogical theories of reality, family therapy is returning to its roots in philosophy to redefine the notion of reality itself. It is my central argument in this book that meaningful reality is a construction, and the way in which we construct reality is by a particular use of analogical language. This way of using language reflects an evolution in the function of language. With analogical language, we construct analogical models or reflections of reality which make up the world in which we live.

The world of a previous epoch was described by means of language used referentially, in what Bateson and Jackson called a digital mode of communication. Language was thought to be distinct from what it represented. The map of language, like a cartographer's map, represented a territory that existed independently. Truth was thought to be the correspondence between words and things that existed independently from words. For philosophers of positivism, who dominated the scene in the first half of the twentieth century, language and reality were distinct classes of logical types. To confuse word and thing, performance and reality, was to make a mistake in logical types, a "category mistake." It did not matter that poets and dramatists made such category mistakes all the time. Literature was thought to be merely *mimesis*, a kind of second-rate imitation of the real world. Literary forms and the forms of objective reality were thought to be quite distinct. Reality was not yet viewed as a text, a creation of language. Analogical communication was still a handmaiden of digital communication, an inferior mode of representing reality. Aesthetics and its constructions were subservient to positivist science as a means for representing what was objective and real. In a distinction first formulated by Aristotle, poetics was sharply differentiated from science and from metaphysics. To deny the difference between map and territory was, as Bateson put it, to enter the "dim region" of art, magic, religion, and play (1972). But it is precisely this "dim region" that is now becoming illuminated as the region of *culture*, in its dynamic aspects as performances and expressions, myth and language. And philosophers since Cassirer are beginning to take seriously the link between cultural forms and reality.

MIRRORS AND REALITY

With the passing of time, the function of language has evolved. Language, in the postmodern era, no longer merely represents; it signifies. The world in which we live appears to us in a mirror of signs. In the world view of a previous epoch, when sign and thing were detached, literature was compared to a mirror which reflected a preexisting reality. To hold a mirror up to nature, including human nature, presumed that nature and human nature existed already, waiting to be reflected. The mirror images produced by art and literature were merely reflections of a preexisting world. Artistic representation was *mimesis*. The image, from this point of view, was an inferior sort of reality, a mere copy or imitation, not the real thing. This idea has its origin in the discussion of art and imitation in the tenth book of Plato's *Republic*, where the images created by the artist are condemned as third-rate imitations of reality. The activity of the artist is likened to someone walking around with a mirror and reflecting the natural world, then presenting the mirror reflections as true reality. The artist, like the sophist, conjures a vivid impression in people's minds which does not, according to Plato, correspond to what is real, permanent, and unchanging.

But our postmodern world lacks the unity of the world of the Greek golden age. In our world, it is the mirrors of language and culture that construct what reality we have. The copy or model of reality, the image, far from being a mere reflection of something else, is all of reality that we have got. For it is, to use Geertz's apt and timely phrase, "the copying that originates." Cultural forms do not, as Geertz (1986) puts it, "mirror" something else in another place which they express metaphorically. Cultural forms are, rather, "the thing itself." The mirror of signs is a very different kind of mirror than the piece of polished glass or still pool of water that Plato's analogy brings to mind. It is a magic mirror of creativity. This view of image and reality, somewhat disconcertingly, turns Plato's analogy on its head. The illusion for our time is that a real world exists ready-made, permanent, and unchanging — waiting to be reflected.

But the world of reflections is not without its perils. The postmodern world is a place in which the dark-souled sophist, whom Plato characterized as a master of manipulating images through language, is most at home. Our world abounds with false realities created by language, which Francis Bacon wisely identified as "idols of the marketplace."

The great literary meta-texts of our century — texts like *Ulysses* and *Waiting for Godot* — heralded the epoch of the signifying power of language in constructing reality. These works are mirrors which teach us, not a little painstakingly, how we in fact construct multiple realities from a shifting text of ambiguous signs. The worlds constructed in these works through language and its forms are mirrors, in which we see, first of all, ourselves. These worlds are, moreover, mirrors of *process*, the constructive or creative process of language organizing chaos. The narrative form portrays even as it constructs the structure of human reality. To ignore the role of analogical language and signs in constructing reality or, more precisely, realities, is to ignore history and the inevitable tides of change.

CONSTRUCTIVISM

Constructivism, the view that we create or construct reality, seems threatening because it apparently threatens to remove the solid ground from beneath our feet. It would seem to deny what is objective and enduring in human life, leaving us in a quicksand of moral ambiguity, equivocation, and flux, in which even our immediate sensations are shaped and conditioned by words and other signs. Cultural constructivism would seem to imply cultural relativism and, even worse, solipsism. Most of us would like to believe, along with Plato, that there are at least unchanging moral values built into the universe, like goodness, courage, loyalty, and truthfulness, which do not shift and change with the sands of history and do not depend upon societies and groups to construct them. This, I propose, is a naive and dangerous way of thinking in the postmodern world. If there is goodness, which surely there is, then it too is a construction in the mirror of signs, tied to polysemic language and narrative forms for its creation and preservation. The continuous constructing and reconstructing of good and evil is preserved in narrative creations such as myths, stories, novels, dramas, folk tales, legends, fairy tales and religious tales. "Listen to our Jewish tales," Elie Wiesel tells us, "and you will know what hurts your friend."

CULTURE

Cultural constructivism does not deny harsh physical realities like earthquakes, floods, political torture, illness, poverty, and hunger. But for the cultural constructivist, reality is *lived* reality, experience shaped by the deep forces of culture. Constructivist reality consists of *events which signify, events which bear meaning in a human experiential context*. There is a difference, as Turner pointed out, between *"mere* experience" and *"an* experience," the former being the passive endurance of events and the latter an experience that stands out, that has meaning and significance in a context, like a rock in a Zen sand garden. For example, an earthquake or flood as *"an* experience" may signify divine retribution. As *"mere* experience" the earthquake or flood is passively endured.

Political torture may have significance as a chapter in the ongoing history of Christian martyrs who died for ideals. Poverty may signify a preparation for death and rebirth into a more elevated state of being, or a preparation for the rewards of eternal life in heaven. A human, lived world is a world in which events are not merely endured, but also may be "read" as ambiguous signs, pregnant with multiple significance and embedded in ongoing narratives that stretch to the past and the future. And in the very ambiguity of events are contained the seeds of hope, of new possibilities. The constructivist is concerned with events that have meaning, meaning diversely construed and richly interpreted by a myriad of groups and societies. Natural events, especially when they are extreme, are multivocal signs, richly significant in human, social contexts.

Constructivism offers not merely the despair of equivocation but also the promise of hope for new possibilities. As the philosopher Ernst Cassirer remarked earlier this century, the world we construct with signs is a phase in the process of the human being's progressive liberation. For in the process of using symbols and signs, Cassirer tells us, "man discovers and proves a new power — the power to build up a world of his own" (1970, p.252).

THEORY AND PRACTICE

Bringing the theory of signs and signification to bear on family therapy has value only if it is useful in a practical way. The family therapist deals with real families and real human problems. The therapist's goals are to ease human suffering, to protect children, women, the impoverished, and other vulnerable groups against abuse and violence, to help people live meaningful, productive lives. Therapy is often the only source of hope to families shadowed by violence and poverty. In an eloquent critique of constructivism, pioneer family therapist Salvador Minuchin (1991) queries poignantly:

> How could it be good therapy to tell a Salvadoran mother whose eldest son has been "disappeared" by a right-wing death squad that the members of her family were self-determining cocreators of their own narratives? (p.49)

I would answer that the *only* good therapy for this woman is a therapy which gives her son's disappearance meaning and significance in her own cultural context, whatever her cultural context happens to be. Such a therapy might, for example, help this mother understand her son's story as a story of heroic Christian martyrdom, framing her son's story among other stories of heroic self-sacrifice for cherished ideals, of stories that give hope to humanity. It might encourage her to connect in collective symbolic acts and commemorative celebrations with other mothers whose family members have been similarly martyred. These are only examples of the many possible ways such a woman may come to construct a meaningful reality, one that gives her pride in her son and hope to go on living.

It is the premise of this book that a therapist can and does effect change in families, and does so by utilizing the signifying and creative power of language. With the realization that events as well as language are signs, therapist and client can construct new realities. Therapy cannot undo atrocious events of the past like sexual abuse and torture. But the meaning of the past as well as the present can be shifted in such a way to create a future that holds hope. It is precisely because human reality *is* ambiguous, because events are signs, open to ever-changing contexts of meaning, that the therapist may help a client create a new story, a new life narrative if you will, by giving new meaning to past and present events interpreted as signs.

THE FUTURE OF FAMILY THERAPY

Family therapies and family therapists differ in many ways, but their mirrors are beginning to converge, especially with respect to the creative role of language. A search for similarity and the initiation of conversation between strategic and narrative family therapies, for example, would strengthen and enrich the field. These two schools of therapy of course have their differences, but they also have many fundamental similarities. Both strategic and narrative therapists reject the traditional diagnostic categories and stigmatizing labels of the dominant narrative or prevailing paradigm of Western culture. Both therapies describe problems and symptoms operationally in nontechnical language, in a way such that potential solutions may become apparent. The focus is on the present and future rather than on the past, on future solutions to problems rather than on uncovering past causes. Both strategic and narrative therapists draw upon the analogical and signifying power of language to construct reality, using metaphors and stories to create therapeutic change. Both schools of therapy have a conception of the self as a social being, with symptoms arising in and reflecting problematic social contexts. The conception of the self in both approaches is an ambiguous, contextual self, extending beyond the boundaries of the physical entity of the person. People are no longer viewed as objective "entities" like rocks or billiard balls. As Jackson (1968), observed in the early years of family therapy, an individual seems less like an "object" and more like a "field of force" extending from intrapsychic processes to the broadest aspects of his cultural milieu. The new conception of the self that is currently emerging in both the strategic and narrative schools of family therapy is a self with blurred edges. It is a self which extends beyond the skin of the individual person to include broader and broader social contexts. This expanded notion of the self is a familiar one to anthropologists. Geertz has remarked (1973) that the Western conception of the person as a bounded center of awareness and action is "a rather peculiar idea" for the rest of the world's cultures. And family therapists who, as Minuchin has reminded us, must also be anthropologists, are beginning to broaden their understanding of the self as well.

The original innovative step of bringing whole families into treatment is now extending even further as family therapists must deal with ever larger social systems in which the individual self is embedded. The self appears as a point of intersection of diverse forces — family, culture, politics, economics, and history. It is a self in which collective as well as individual memories must be taken into account. The self that postmodern therapy has come to construct is, I suggest, the self as a multivocal sign, a "semiotic self," to borrow a fertile phrase from the semiotician Thomas Sebeok. The semiotic self, Sebeok reminds us, "is by no means identical with the consciousness that binds our life together" (1991). It is a self that is essentially contextual. Fulfilling the Delphic injunction "know thyself" may be the task of more than a single lifetime.

POWER

Power has been a much disputed topic in the field of family therapy. Strategic therapy from its origins had a concern with power and hierarchy in relationships, and many of its directives are aimed at redistributing power and changing hierarchies in families. The therapist attempts to bring about a situation in which parents are in charge of their children, not vice versa. It is also a central idea of strategic therapy that the therapist-patient hierarchy must be clearly defined in order for the family hierarchy to be correct. The therapist avoids making coalitions with children against their parents, thus raising their status in the family hierarchy. Similarly, the hierarchical arrangement between therapist and supervisor is reflected in the relation of therapist and client. If the therapist trusts and follows the directions of his supervisor, the client is more likely to trust and follow the directions of the therapist.

Narrative therapy, although it seeks to deemphasize power and hierarchy because of the potential for these to be oppressive, still maintains important hierarchical boundaries in the therapist-client relationship. For example, the narrative therapist presents his clients with diplomas, certificates, and awards (White & Epston, 1990). In these acts, the narrative therapist overtly defines himself in a position of power and authority vis-à-vis the client. In most contexts of human social interaction, it is the teacher, the authority figure, who presents the student with a certificate of achievement, not vice versa. Although the narrative therapist is no longer an *omniscient* narrator, he still has a privileged place in the story.

Power, like much else in the postmodern world, is a polysemic sign with a double edge. Power may be used for good, when it is infused with respect for other human beings as ends-in-themselves, or for evil, when it is used to oppress, to put down, to use other people as means toward one's own selfish ends. It is important not to confuse power with a directive style in therapy. A therapist may be directive yet gentle, strategic yet caring, competent and effective yet respectful of the human dignity of her clients. Paradoxical strategies, when they are used skillfully and benevolently, are powerful tools to relieve human suffering. In the hands of an unskilled or unethical therapist, however, these strategies have the power to cause harm.

To say that the therapist is being consulted in her position as an expert in solving family problems is not to say that she looks down on a client as somehow damaged or inferior to herself. One consults a therapist for her expertise in solving problems that people have in a way that is analogous to consulting an automobile mechanic for his expertise in solving problems that cars have. The mechanic does not think less of a car because it has a problem. A client may in fact have an expertise superior to that of the therapist in another domain. She may be an expert in her own field, in science, in business, or in the arts. But the client is coming to therapy because she trusts that the therapist has expertise in solving certain kinds of human problems, an area of expertise that the client does not have. A therapist's power, like that of any professional, can be oppressive, manipulative, and undesirable when it is not combined with benevolence and respect. A therapist has the obligation to respect the human dignity of the client and the dignity of other professionals who may be part of the client's or her own broader social context. In the postmodern world we are both agents and objects of our actions. The therapist who compulsively abuses, puts down, and demeans other people would do well to reconstruct this story, lest she, like Beckett's Estragon, discover that in trying to harm others she succeeds only in harming herself.

In a therapy that is based upon constructivist ideas, there is room for pluralism and for mutual respect. The approach taken in this book is essentially pluralistic and nondogmatic, in the spirit of pluralism and constructivism that is part of the philosophical legacy of John Dewey and the other American pragmatists. There are many stories and many hypotheses that can explain an event or a situation, and there are many possible constructions of reality. The preference for one story or one construction over another depends on the goal of the inquiry and the purpose or intention of the inquirer. The attitude of pluralism requires a decentering or detachment from our own viewpoint, our own construction, so that we may recognize the viewpoints of others even if we do not choose them for ourselves. The test of a theory of therapy is not its objective truth, but its *viability* or *effectiveness* in solving the vast diversity of problems for which people consult therapists today.

CHAPTER 2

The Mirror of Signs

Half asleep (on the plane) I looked out into the night and saw my father's face looking in squinting, trying to see something. I sat up. But of course it was my own face, my reflection in the glass squinting, trying to see something looking out.

— Michael J. Arlen

THIS BOOK ADDRESSES a basic philosophical issue in postmodern family therapy: whether we have contact with objective reality, or whether, at this phase in the tide of history, we live in a world of our own constructions. I take the latter point of view, and propose that we construct reality by means of signs in a problem-solving context. The belief that there is a fixed reality, ready-made and eternal, "behind" our cultural constructions, our signs, is an illusion, albeit a persistent illusion. What we have of reality are reflections in the mirror of signs. Human reality is thus a dynamic process, a process in constant creation. In this chapter, I provide a philosophical and historical context for this position.

A related issue is the locus of the family therapist — whether or not the therapist is intrinsically part of the family system, and if she is, what the implications of this are for effecting change in the system. My usage of the term "family system" goes beyond the usual connotations of the term in the family therapy literature. I am using the notion of a system as existing only through the participation of a therapist-observer. Just as, in quantum mechanics, the wave form of a particle collapses to a single observable state upon observation, so a social group coalesces into a system upon observation. The therapist cannot assume that a family system exists apart from the act of observation any more than the quantum physicist can assume a particle maintains a particular state before or after the act of observation.

The family system the therapist constructs for the purpose of therapy is somewhat arbitrary, varying from case to case. The system may consist of children and their parents, or children, parents, and grandparents. At times the therapist may have to consider teachers, friends, aunts, uncles, or godparents as part of the system in order to resolve the problem brought to therapy. Foster parents, social workers, representatives of the judicial system—all of these play increasingly larger roles in the lives of clients who come to therapy and must at times be considered as part of the client's social context. The assemblage of persons that constitutes a family "system," therefore, depends on the particular purpose at hand: the problem to be solved and finding the most effective solution to that problem.

Just as a system depends for its meaning on an observer, so also a symptom, a person, or a sequence of interaction can be a sign or metaphor only with reference to an observer and the purpose of the observation. The reality that we construct with signs is rooted in our intention or purpose. For example, often a therapist may find it useful to see a child's symptom as a metaphor for a parent's situation (Haley, 1976; Madanes, 1981). The therapist who uses metaphor in conceptualizing a problematic situation need not assume the "true" existence of this metaphorical relation apart from the purposes and processes of therapy. Truth and falsehood, which are qualities of the constructions of digital communication, are not applicable when we are discussing analogical models. Metaphorical sequences in families, although they seem to have a life of their own, are only useful constructions or stories that we create to help us solve family problems.

METAPHOR: A CASE EXAMPLE

A six-year-old girl is in my office with her mother. The girl has been having painful stomachaches and hasn't been able to go to school for several weeks. The child's pediatrician has told me that she cannot find a medical cause for the girl's stomachaches. After talking with the child and her mother for a few minutes I learn that mother and father have recently divorced and mother is living a somewhat isolated existence. From this, I construct the hypothesis that the daughter's stomachache is a metaphor or sign for the emotional upset in her mother's life. I also hypothesize that the stomachaches serve a protective function in the family system. If the child has a stomachache, she can stay home from school and her mother does not have to be alone all day.

I arrange a dramatic game as a kind of experiment to test my hypothesis. I ask mother and daughter to change roles for a game of "pretending."[1] I ask mother to pretend she is having a stomachache, and daughter is to comfort her with hugs and kisses and soothing words. She may want to bring mother a cup of tea from the kitchen off my waiting room. I notice that the child is very eager to take on this role of comforting her mother and performs her part well. I comment that she is mommy's little helper, and her eyes fill with tears. She recognizes that I have understood the reason for the stomachaches, even though the girl herself could not have articulated it. I tell the child that from now on she is to be mommy's helper in a new way. They are to perform the drama of pretending three times a day at home, before and after school and in the evening. Daughter is to comfort mother with hugs and kisses and homemade get well cards for her pretend illness. In the child's presence I make an appointment to meet with mother alone, to help her cope with the transition of divorce and create a new life for herself. In an aside, I tell the child that I will be mommy's helper now, and her job is to go to school and do well. A few weeks later the girl's stomachaches are gone and she is back at school.

This scene has been reenacted in my office countless times with

---

[1]This strategy was created by Cloé Madanes. Further discussion of the strategy of "pretending" may be found in Madanes, 1981, 1984.

a great variety of children's and adolescent's symptoms, from stomachaches and headaches to delinquency and anorexia nervosa. Viewing the symptom as an analogical expression or metaphor is useful in such a case because it directs me from the stomachaches to the mother's loneliness, which I can do something about by helping mother reorganize during a transitional period in her life. Viewing the child's symptom as having a protective function in a mother-daughter system enables me to invent a strategy to stop the stomachaches and get the child back to school.

By providing new ways of helping mother, I free the daughter from having to communicate analogically with a symptom. I will spend several sessions with mother helping her establish a network of support so that she doesn't have to be alone while her daughter is at school. I may orient her toward going back to college where she will make new friendships, or toward finding a job. I may help her reconnect with her family of origin. Perhaps I will encourage her to arrange a social event with one of her daughter's classmates and her mother. Which of these interventions I choose depends on what comes up in my conversations with mother, what interests she has and her motivations. Once the child has communicated to me the meaning of her symptom, I can work on finding a healthier solution to the problem the child has been attempting to solve in an unfortunate way.

A MODEL OF REALITY

An apparent paradox presents itself. If my hypothesis about the protective function of the symptom in the system is correct, the pretending exercise with mother will work to effect change in the system. The child will improve in a few sessions. If my hypothesis is incorrect — for example, if the child's symptom refers not to mother but to father or to grandmother — then her symptom will not improve until I extend the system to include father or grandmother and involve him or her in the therapy. In some sense, then, the metaphorical connection of daughter and mother seems to pre-exist my articulating it and puts certain constraints on the model I construct. But this apparent paradox is resolved if we consider the essentially practical nature of therapy. The touchstone of my

constructed reality is not a state of affairs external to the context
of therapy. The touchstone is the *effectiveness* of the model of
reality I construct in solving the problem at hand in therapy. My
hypothesis, or the reality that I construct, is proved or disproved
by the results. The question becomes whether working with a particular hypothesis produces the desired change in the system — that
is, whether the child's symptom disappears. If one hypothesis does
not lead to change, then it must be discarded and another hypothesis taken up and tried.

Assuming that symptoms have a protective function, however
useful this is to doing effective therapy, is not a statement about
what is in fact true in the traditional sense of the word "truth." The
statement does not claim to represent a preexisting reality or state
of affairs. Nor do we bring in the notion of "causality," an important rule in the grammar of digital communication but not very
helpful in analogical systems. We do not speculate about whether
the child *actually* plans to help a parent by having a symptom. We
may say, as Madanes (1981) does, that the symptom is "as if"
planned. The child's symptom and the mother's situation are reciprocal or mutually reflective.

In the postmodern world, all that we know of human social
reality, and quite arguably of natural reality, are models or reflections. The system I construct with my hypothesis of protection is
only one among many reflections of social reality that may be
created in therapy. As societies evolve and the problems of societies
change, different mirrors of the human psyche, soul, or spirit become particularly relevant to conceptualizing and solving problems. The question of whether one model is as good as another
comes down to which model most effectively leads to a solution for
the problem at hand. As we shall see, this attitude of mind has
many similarities to the philosophical standpoint of American
pragmatism.

The family therapist Mara Palazzoli takes a similar position on
the role of theoretical constructions in the practice of therapy:

> I also know that my model of the family game is my own
> construction. I know that there are many stories, but I
> worked for ten years to construct this story. I work as if

my model is true even though I'm sure that nobody knows
what reality is. But, if with this road map I can repeatedly
be confirmed by the family and arrive at success, maybe
we are near *a* true story, but not *the* true story. (Simon,
1987, p.30)

So it is with the story or hypothesis of the protective function of
the symptom in a family system. Like Palazzoli's useful construction of a family "game," the hypothesis of protectiveness guides the
therapist to help families solve serious problems. Because it has led
to many successful resolutions of problems, it is therefore one true
story, though not *the* true story.

REFLEXIVITY

In hypothesizing that a symptom is a metaphor and that a symptom has a function in a family system, the therapist is in a sense
constructing both the metaphorical relation and the system. And in
doing this the therapist is creating himself as a part of his creation.
He is both agent and object. In the case of metaphor, the therapist
is an agent, the one *through which* the daughter's symptom refers
to or signifies her mother's pain. Without the therapist making the
connection, the link between sign and signified does not exist. The
significance of the stomachache has not been communicated to
anyone. A triadic relation that involves the mind of the interpreter
of the sign is required for a meaningful sign to exist. In the case of
the new system, in which the therapist takes over the protective
role, thereby eliminating the need for the symptom, the therapist
becomes a part of a mother-daughter-therapist triad. The system
created by the therapist is in this sense reflexive, bearing its creator,
as object, within it. The therapist, as author of the constructed
reality, becomes a character in it as well. He is, paradoxically, both
agent and object.

POLYSEMIC LANGUAGE

In my simple example of a girl with a stomachache, I have used
metaphor in another sense. In telling the child that she is her moth-

er's "helpcr," I am apparently referring to the make-believe drama in which mother pretends to have a stomachache and daughter helps by soothing and comforting her. But I am also referring to the child's having stomachaches in order to stay home from school and keep her mother company, thereby protecting mother. Thirdly, the child as her mother's "helper" has yet another obvious meaning. She is providing a reason for mother to consult a therapist. When I use the word "helper" metaphorically, the child understands me because she feels this to be so, although perhaps she could not have put it into words. In general, the older the child the more able she is to perceive the construct of the protective function of the symptom.

In using the word "helper" as a metaphor, I am drawing on the *polysemic* or *multivocal* quality of words. *Polysemic*, derived from Greek, means "many signed," and *multivocal*, from Latin, means "many voiced." This use of language is most familiar in poetry. But, as we shall see, polysemy or multivocality has wider implications as the power of language to create or construct reality.

In using the word "helper" in a polysemic way I am also constructing a relation between mother and daughter, in which one is the helper and the other the helped. I then construct a system in which I stand in the same relation to the mother as the daughter previously stood. I become helper to the mother. I am creating relations between what had been unconnected occurrences.

THE THEORY OF SIGNS

A metaphor is a type of sign. In order to get a better understanding of metaphor, we must look more closely at the nature of signs. The study of signs, which is called semiotics, provides us with a useful tool for understanding the way in which we build constructions of reality. Using the language of Charles Sanders Peirce, the originator of the modern theory of signs, a metaphor is a particular type of sign which he called an *icon*. Icon comes from the Greek word *eikon*, which means image or reflection. The scope of this chapter does not allow for a discussion of the three types of signs and their subgenres, which Peirce identified, and the distinct characteristics of icons, indices, and symbols. Rather, I shall limit the discussion to iconic signs in a general sense. A metaphor, or iconic sign, is a sign because it signifies or refers to something other than itself. It refers to some thing, in some respect, as perceived by some observer. In my example, the girl's stomach ache is a sign because it refers to the girl's mother, with respect to pain, as observed by or communicated to the therapist. The system I construct by interpreting a symptom or problem as a metaphor of another problem is a system of signs, constructed by the triadic relation of metaphor, object, and interpretant. A physician may interpret the stomachache as another type of sign, as, say, a sign of the flu or of indigestion. In this case the sign would be, in Peirce's language, an *index* instead of an *icon*.

For a sign to have any meaning whatsoever, an observing mind, or what Peirce called the *interpretant* of the sign, must make a connection between sign and signified in a particular context. Whether the context is family therapy or medicine makes a great deal of difference as to what signs will be perceived. Peirce emphasized that a sign always involves a *triadic* relation of sign, signified and interpretant. Apart from the context of therapy, the stomachache in my example does not signify the pain of the child's mother. It is simply a stomachache, a physical pain. It is the aspect of the stomachache as iconic sign, not as physical reality, that the therapist focuses on for the purpose of effecting change.

Semiotics is instructive to family therapy for at least three reasons: First, semiotics includes the *observer* essentially in the perception of any metaphorical or signifying relation. Second, semiotics ties the goal of any inquiry to the *problem* the inquirer is attempting to solve. Science or any other inquiry is essentially *purposive* or intentional. Third, the relations of signs, including language as a system of signs, *reflect* or *mirror* reality. But they do not (and this is of critical importance) represent a preexisting reality. Signs are not iconic in the traditional sense of picturing an object already formed. Reflecting is creating, making, bringing into existence. It is of a poetic process, in the original sense of the word *poesis,* which simply meant "making." Objects come into existence with the construction of the sign by the observer. Objects do not exist ready-made.

Peirce (1897/1955) expressed the first idea by saying that the relation of sign, object, and interpretant is genuinely "triadic" and does not consist of any "complexus of dyadic relations." In other words, a sign is significant only in relation to an observer-interpretant. Without an interpretant, a sign is, so to speak, just a sign. Peirce pointed out that signs are by their very nature ambiguous, for a sign may have any number of objects. The way in which we interpret a sign and create an object depends on the goals and experience of the inquirer.

PRAGMATISM AND REALITY

Peirce was a pragmatist philosopher, in an American philosophical tradition that included John Dewey, William James, and George Herbert Mead. Peirce was the most eccentric of the four and distinguished his particular brand of pragmatism from the others by calling his philosophical position "pragmaticism." However, Peirce shared many important ideas with the other pragmatists. William James defined pragmatism in a threefold way: as an attitude of mind, a theory of ideas and truth, and a theory about reality. As an attitude, James said, pragmatism looked away from first principles and "supposed necessities" and toward future outcomes and consequences. Facts are defined as the fruits or products of inquiry. They are not out there in the world waiting for us to discover them. As a theory of truth, pragmatism was concerned with solving problems rather than ascertaining truth, in the traditional sense of truth as a correspondence between our ideas and a preexisting factual reality. For the pragmatist, the goal of any inquiry is practical. It is a solution to a problem in the world. A true idea is defined as an idea that works in achieving the goal of the inquiry. Finally, pragmatism had a conception of reality, of the very structure of the universe, as continuously in the process of unfolding rather than as static and fixed for all eternity. As James articulated it, this was a view that reality was "still in the making," as opposed to the belief that "there is an eternal edition of it ready-made and complete" (Dewey, 1916, p.305). Peirce's theory of signs sprang up in the context of pragmatism's method of scientific inquiry. Peirce (1878/1955) valued pragmatism as a philosophical position precisely because of its recognition of the connection between knowledge and purpose.

We find a similar attitude in the school of family therapy known as strategic family therapy. Haley (1976) was perhaps the first to propose that therapy is essentially a problem-solving activity. A therapist works with analogical or metaphorical communications in a problem-solving context. The goal of finding an effective and timely solution for a problem shapes the way the therapist perceives a situation and shapes the hypothesis or story he formulates to describe the situation. In a very real sense, the goal of problem-solving shapes the very reality that the therapist sees in front of him. The meanings the therapist attributes to events and the way he punctuates sequences of events in patterns are inextricably tied to the way he conceives the problem he is attempting to solve.

Another important contribution from Peirce concerning the nature of inquiry is his notion of validity. For Peirce (1896/1955), science was not the royal road to truth. Instead, he believed the power of science was to approximate indefinitely toward truth, through constantly evolving modes of perception and reasoning. Reality is essentially a matter of opinion, belief, or faith. It is what would be agreed upon by an infinite number of investigators, if there could ever be a point at which investigation stops. What is real, according to Peirce, is never fully revealed. It represents merely a hope or an idea projected into the future.

Thomas Kuhn (1970), in describing the evolution of science in his classic work, *The Structure of Scientific Revolutions*, comes to a similar conclusion.

> There is, I think, no theory-independent way to reconstruct phrases like "really there"; the notion of a match between the ontology of a theory and its "real" counterpart in nature now seems to me illusive in principle. (p.206)

For Kuhn, the essence of science is puzzle-solving, not the progressive evolution toward an objective, true account of what nature "really" is. A new paradigm gains ascendency over an old one not because it gets closer to a description of reality, but because it provides solutions to problems that that the old paradigm cannot solve. Kuhn argues that there is no absolute truth about any particular paradigm of science. Kuhn also maintains that scientific knowledge, like language, is the common property of a group of scientists. To understand science, he writes, "we need to know the special characteristic of the groups that create and use it" (1970, p.210). Kuhn ultimately arrived at a relativist position as to the meaning of science, for which his book was strongly attacked. But he held his ground, asserting that "if the position be relativism, I cannot see that the relativist loses anything needed to account for the nature and development of the sciences" (p.207).

Kuhn's idea that science is puzzle-solving provides a useful analogy for what therapy is. Although it is an art not a science, therapy is essentially puzzle-solving. A therapist may interpret a situation in any number of ways—he may construct any number of realities to explain it—with no one interpretation being verifiable as more valid absolutely than another. Validity resides in the utility of the assumption in solving the problem of inquiry. Not every therapist, not even therapists with similar backgrounds and training, will perceive the same metaphors in a situation. Also, just as there are many stories or models that describe a situation brought to therapy, so are there many solutions. The idea of the symptom having a protective function is one model, one story among many. The strategy of correcting the family hierarchy to solve problems of delinquency and schizophrenia is another useful model or story. If, as Palazzoli has pointed out, one model is repeatedly confirmed by successful change in the family, the therapist has a model that is useful. As times change and new problems emerge in families and in society, any particular model of therapy may cease to be useful.

ABDUCTION

Seeing a symptom as a metaphor or an iconic sign requires training in a particular way of seeing. Where one therapist who has been trained in using metaphor may perceive a daughter's symptom as a metaphor for a depressed mother, another therapist with different training may not. Another therapist might, for example, see the stomachache as an hysterical symptom referring to a traumatic past event such as sexual abuse. With this hypothesis, the questions the therapist asks and the whole way he conducts the therapy would be very different from that of a therapist using the model of the symptom as protective. The model used by each, including above all the goal and intent of inquiry, *shapes* the reality he seems to discover. The *meaning* of things has to do with the attitude of the inquirer. Meaning is emergent, not fixed in the structure of events. The inquiring mind and what seems to be "external reality" are in this sense mutually reflective.

This mode of constructing a useful hypothesis to guide inquiry is a method that Peirce (1901/1955) called abduction, which he defines as a "preference for any one hypothesis over others which would equally explain the facts" (p.151). The preferable hypothesis is the one that gets the inquirer to the goal of the inquiry. In the context of problem-solving therapy, it is the hypothesis that guides one to solving the problem presented.

A MIRRORED REALITY

An example from Peirce (1897/1955) illustrates what he means by the way in which we come to know an object by a sign.

> Two men are standing on the seashore looking out to sea. One of them says to the other, "That vessel there carries no freight at all, but only passengers." Now if the other, himself, sees no vessel, the first information he derives from the remark has for its object the part of the sea that he does see, and informs him that a person with sharper eyes than his, or more trained in looking for such things, can see a vessel there; and then, that vessel having been thus introduced to his acquaintance, he is prepared to receive the information about it that it carries passengers exclusively. But the sentence as a whole has, for the person supposed, no other Object than that with which it finds him already acquainted. (p.101)

The reality constructed by signs — like the passenger vessel in this subtle example — does not admit of what Peirce calls "firsthand acquaintance." It is an abstract kind of reality that is known only through reflections. It is tied to an orientation of mind toward an object just beyond the viewer's horizon, presently invisible, but nonetheless known to be there because its presence is communicated by signs. Whatever else may be said about the object, our only acquaintance with it is through signs, through analogies. The way a sign is related to its object, through an interpretant, mirrors a dynamic reality in the process of creation, a reality, as James put it, "still in the making." Peirce's (1897/1955) theory of signs, which he equates with *logic*, provides us, on the one hand, with a logic of analogical communication and, on the other, with a poetics of reality.

This reflective point of view does not deny the reality of the physical world, the world of nature. Physical objects and events are real, but they are also signs. They make us aware of a dimmer and more elusive object, which we, like the second man on the seashore, cannot quite grasp at first. In a similar vein, mind reflects a natural world. To put it another way, to say "there is a special providence in the fall of a sparrow" does not deny the sparrow's trajectory. But the significance of the statement is that it moves the mind to a different level of discourse in which visible events *may* be read as signifying that which is not visible. As the semiotician Thomas Sebeok (1991) tells us: "there are objects and signs of objects, the former also being signs but used in a different way" (p.51).

SYMPTOMS AS SIGNS

Let us now move to the application of the theory of signs to the practice of therapy. Viewing a symptom as a sign does not negate the physical reality of the symptom. A stomachache may signify another type of pain, but it is still a stomachache, a physical pain. And the goal of therapy is to remove the pain. In a case of a young girl with symptoms of anorexia, for example, I may hypothesize that the symptoms are signs. They may, from my point of view, signify the emotional starvation of the girl's mother or of the relation between mother and father. But I also see the girl's physical body in front of me, dangerously close to starvation. And I measure the progress of therapy by how many physical pounds the girl gains each week. However, I conduct the therapy by viewing the symptoms as relational or interactional rather than individual. I view the symptoms as protective (the daughter has brought her parents to therapy) and as signs of the family's emotional, sexual, and spiritual starvation. And I address myself to solving the latter problems, meeting with the parents and the family, in order to cure the girl's anorexia.

LANGUAGE: FROM REPRESENTATION
TO SIGNIFICATION

The postmodern notion of reality represents a shift from the attitude of uncovering physical events that have "caused" a client's problem to one in which the therapist constructs a hypothesis about what is analogically *signified* by the problem or symptom. That is to say, the postmodern therapist is concerned with *meaning*. Let us take the example of sexual abuse of children, which has been such a critically important problem for therapy from the beginning. After treating a number of patients with symptoms of the neurosis that he called "hysteria," Freud came to the conclusion that all neurotic symptoms were rooted in instances of actual sexual seduction during the patient's infancy or childhood. Some years later, he changed his mind and decided that he had initially overestimated the frequency of the occurrences of actual seduction of children. He concluded that although *some* hysterical symptoms originated in actual seductions of the patient by adults or older children, most hysterical symptoms stemmed from patients' fantasies of sexual seduction. Freud candidly admitted that he had had difficulty discriminating between "deceptive memories" and "memory traces" of actual occurrences. Freud called the fantasies "defenses," which served to mask memories of actual autoerotic activities of the child (Freud, 1905). Because the autoerotic acts became associated with shameful feelings in the child's mind, Freud believed that the mind disguised them as fantasies, thus defending itself from the painful feeling of shame.

Even when he changed his mind about the cause of neuroses from actual *occurrences* of sexual seduction to *fantasies* of sexual seduction, Freud still used the model of objective physical events in the past which therapy sought to uncover. Fantasies symbolized objectively real events. The therapist, somewhat like an archeologist, excavated the psyche to get at hidden past events. By interpreting fantasy and dream symbols correctly, Freud believed that the therapist could uncover "real" events in the past, behind the mental constructions.

What I am proposing is that the notion of "reality" has evolved. Or, to say the same thing differently, our modes of perception and expression have evolved. The reality of the postmodern therapist is very different from the reality of Freud's historical times. One way of expressing this difference is to say that for Freud signs and symbols *represented* a preexisting set of material facts that constituted reality. Signs and symbols were interpreted with the goal of revealing a hard reality beneath them. For the postmodern therapist, however, reality has become the dependent variable. Reality is constructed in the dynamic process of interaction between the problem-solving therapist and the client. Distinguishing deceptive memories from real memories of sexual abuse is no less difficult now than it was for Freud. But the question for therapy is the *significance* of the remembered sexual abuse, real or fantasized, in the client's present experience. The past is not severed inextricably from the present and present experience. A memory of abuse may be the shoals upon which a family breaks apart, or the disclosure of abuse may provide a new source of open communication and connection for a family, as we shall see in a later chapter of this book.

SIGNIFICATION

Let us return to Peirce's idea that signs and their relations mirror an object not directly observable. In Peirce's view, a sign generates a relation in the mind of the observer between itself and its object, which is an ever-receding reality, never fully revealed, but tied, like a Siren and her song, to the signs that portray it. This idea that reality is constructed or reflected by signs has a parallel in a particular function of language. Language, which is a system of signs, has not only the function of representing; it also *signifies*. Language does not merely represent a preexisting object, but may also signify an object by moving the observer's mind to a particular orientation. Saussure referred to the signifying aspect of language as *"sig-*

The Mirror of Signs

nificativite" or *"pouvoir de signifier"* (Sebeok, 1991, p.152). Language, for Saussure, is not a referential or denotative system. Meaning is created from the relationships among signs. Cassirer (1970), similarly, refers to the "energy" of language, its "constructive" or signifying aspect, as opposed to a merely "reproductive" or copying function (p.145).

One of the more interesting questions raised by semiotics or the theory of signs is whether signs (including language) and their structures *reflect* an underlying reality or whether the structures of signs themselves *create* the reality (Sebeok, 1991). This distinction is analogous to the question of whether language represents or signifies. This book takes the latter position—namely that reality is the dependent variable, tied to signs and their structures. This position is in a sense an idealism, which maintains that all reality, even the data of perception, depends to a large extent upon constructions of mind. This is the thrust of Peirce's insistence on the necessity for an interpretant, on the triadic relation inherent in signs. A particular bent of mind mediates the relation between a sign and its object, between signifier and signified, between analogical language and reality.

This view contrasts with positivist or empiricist views of reality as something already fashioned and independent of signs. These theories are known as philosophical realism. The semiotic point of view differs also from various kinds of philosophical idealism or rationalism, which hold that the ideas we have merely mirror a reality that is ready-made and complete in the realm of mind, such as Plato's ideal forms. Peirce's semiotic view is similar to James's and Dewey's conception of a reality that is "still in the making." Ideas, they tell us, guide us in arranging sequences or patterns in events. As Dewey (1916) puts it:

> In other words, as idea is a draft drawn upon existing things and intention to act so as to arrange them in a certain way . . . the meaning of an idea is the changes it, as our attitude, affects in objects. (p.310)

Finally, the semiotic viewpoint is distinct from that of rationalist philosophies, for which the ultimate goal of inquiry is knowledge or insight. The goal of inquiry as the pragmatists conceived of it is practical. Inquiry must lead us to solve concrete problems in concrete situations, to make a difference, as James put it, "to you and me, at definite instants of our life" (Dewey, 1916).

BATESON'S VIEW OF MIND AND REALITY

Gregory Bateson, who also questioned the objectivity or ready-madeness of the universe, addresses from a slightly different angle the question of the mutual reflexivity of the inquiring mind and the natural world that is the object of inquiry. He argues that nature and the human mind are mutually reflective. Bateson (1979) sees nature as a mirror that reflects the highest attributes of the human mind and the human spirit rather than merely the materiality of mankind:

> On the whole, it was not the crudest, the simplest, the most animalistic and primitive aspects of the human species that were reflected in the natural phenomena. It was, rather, the more complex, the aesthetic, the intricate, and the elegant aspects of people that reflected nature. It was not my greed, my purposiveness, my so-called "animal," so-called "instincts," and so forth that I was recognizing on the other side of that mirror, over there in "nature." Rather, I was seeing there the roots of human symmetry, beauty and ugliness, aesthetics, the human being's aliveness and little bit of wisdom. (p.5)

In this idea of Bateson's we find an echo of Kant's notion that to take delight in the sublimity of nature is a sign of moral goodness in a human being. In both these views, there is the suggestion that nature is something more than the hard material realm of facts that science investigates. There is the idea that nature is, at least in part, a construction of mind that mirrors a higher and more noble aspect of humanity. Neither Kant nor Bateson makes an ontological claim for the sublimity of nature. Neither goes so far as to say, as St. Augustine does, that nature actually bears the imprint and signature of a Divine Creator.

LANGUAGE AND REALITY

It has been argued by many philosophers from Rousseau to Cassirer that the laws of nature are nothing other than the laws of language. Rousseau said we are "governed" by the forms of grammar — as though we ourselves were little more than nouns and verbs. Earlier, Francis Bacon had identified the phenomenon of language "governing" the way we perceive reality. He called the realities that men created in their social interactions with one another "idols of the market-place." Bacon writes, in the *Novum Organon*, which was published in 1620, "For men believe that their reason governs words; but it is also true that words react on the understanding" (1620/1955, p.477). Bacon was concerned with the power of words to create in our minds illusory realities, what he called "idols," that do not really exist. He believed that this power of language often stood in the way of our perceiving objective reality. Words, he believed, could refract and distort the clear, pure light of nature from shining through to us in all its clarity. Nature was a book that we must learn to read correctly. Bacon had a pre-Kantian view of nature as independent of the constructions of the human mind. Yet he also perceived the power of words and signs to create an impression of reality in our minds.

THE WEB OF LANGUAGE

Cassirer, in the twentieth century, has an opposite and more optimistic attitude toward the power of words and language to create reality. Cassirer (1957) tells us that language organizes all of our experience and even shapes our very intuitions of ourselves:

> By the same spiritual act through which man spins language out of himself he spins himself into it: so that in the end he communicates and lives with intuitive objects in no other manner than that shown him by the medium of language. (p.15)

For Cassirer, language (and its offspring, myth) should not be thought of as a "veil of *Maya*," obfuscating the pure white light of objective reality, which would otherwise shine through unimpeded to the human mind. For Cassirer, language in its constructive and cultural aspect is viewed as determining what counts as reality in the first place. Experience is patterned in language and in myths. If the reality spun out by language be indeed *Maya*, or illusion, it would seem that the realm of illusion may well be wider than we generally assume.

Cassirer's philosophical position is similar to the semiotic conception of culture in the social sciences which originated, according to Geertz, with Max Weber. At the beginning of his classic paper, "Thick Description: Toward an Interpretive Theory of Culture," Geertz (1973) writes:

> The concept of culture I espouse, and whose utility the essays below attempt to demonstrate, is essentially a semiotic one. Believing, with Max Weber, that man is an animal suspended in webs of significance he himself has spun, I take culture to be those webs, and the analysis of it to be therefore not an experimental science in search of law but an interpretive one in search of meaning. (p.5)

CASSIRER AND THE KANTIAN TRADITION

Cassirer's constructivist view is neo-Kantian, except for the important difference that for Cassirer it is the forms of language and not the forms of thought which organize human experience and construct human reality. An object, according to Cassirer's view, is no longer conceived of as the Kantian object, which is created by concepts joined with perceptions. For Cassirer, objects bear the reflective and spiritual imprint of language, myth, and other cultural forms, prior to becoming organized by conceptual thinking. For Cassirer, objects are inseparable from subjects, but subjects conceived of differently from the thinking subjects that Kant described in *The Critique of Pure Reason* (1781/1929). A deeper and more meaningful experience of reality takes shape not through the Kantian lens of conceptual thinking, but through the cultural lenses of myth and language. For Cassirer, culture with its *mythos* supersedes philosophy with its *logos*.

If Kant may be called a constructivist, as von Glasersfeld does call him (1984), then Kant is a rational constructivist. Von Glasersfeld points out that Vico, more than half a century before Kant, had a constructivist position of a different sort, akin to what I have been describing as cultural constructivism. Of Vico, von Glasersfeld writes:

> He suggests that mythology and art approach the real world by means of symbols. They, too, are made, but the interpretation of their meaning provides a kind of knowledge that is different from the rational knowledge of construction. (p.28)

Vico, unlike Kant, for whom epistemology ultimately replaced ontology, connected his constructivist position to ontology. Von Glasersfeld suggests that Vico takes this step because he is reluctant to stress the independence of man's constructions from those of God. But it is not by means of *rational realism* that Vico links man's creativity to God's. It is by means of the *symbolic modes* of mythology and art.

The philosopher and literary critic Kenneth Burke falls within the tradition of Vico's constructivism. Burke (1968) agrees with Cassirer's definition of man as *homo symbolicum*. For Burke, reality is a construct built up of symbol systems. But he contrasts himself with Cassirer who, "as a post-Kantian gets epistemologically sidetracked" (p.23). Burke's metaphor of the drama, which he uses to describe all of human reality, has, he claims, an ontological status.

KANT'S CONCEPT OF EXPERIENCE

Kant limited the scope of science to what he called the objective reality of nature, which conformed, he proposed, to the universal human processes of conceptual, linear thought and to universal forms of perception. The concepts of the understanding, or categories, and the forms of perception, space, and time, were universal forms that shaped all *experience*. Objective experience has a privileged and narrow status for Kant. Experience is what may be attained by all rational beings, independent of their particular cul-

ture. In the Kantian view, we may have *ideas* that do not have
anything corresponding to them in the natural world, such as the
idea of God or of human freedom. We may think these ideas — in
fact it is inevitable that the human mind will think them — but they
are ideas detached from all physical reality. We may never claim
for these ideas the status of objective experience.

The postmodern thinker, immersed in the ambiguous and, from
a Kantian point of view, merely *subjective* reality constructed by
signs, need not give up the tradition of scientific thinking altogether. What he does need to give up is the world view of Newtonian and post-Kantian science, which presupposed the objective reality of nature and the objective experience of nature. The reality
spun out by Newtonian science presumes a nature at rest, static and
complete. Nature is a book already written.

> In the concepts of space and time, mass and force, action
> and reaction, as defined by Newton, the basic framework
> of physical reality seemed to have been established once
> and for all. (Cassirer, 1957, p.20)

For Kant, the human mind "co-authors," so to speak, the book
of nature. This is no longer Francis Bacon's book of nature, au-
thored by God alone and merely waiting to be read and interpreted
correctly by man, the "servant and interpreter of Nature." For Kant
believed that the logic of the natural world conformed to the logical
forms or categories of the human mind, and to the a priori forms
of perception, space and time. These forms, he believed, were universal and a priori, outside the flow of temporality. In Kant's view,
neither historical process nor "merely subjective" cultural conditions were considered relevant to science or to the universal and
objective reality that was the object of scientific investigation.

CHAPTER 3

The Semiotic Self

When we think . . . we ourselves, as we are at that moment appear as a sign.

Charles Sanders Peirce

IT HAS BECOME EVIDENT to the postmodern mind that reality is neither written and fixed for all eternity (as Bacon believed), nor does reality reflect structures of the human mind that are unchanging and universal (as Kant believed). Reality evolves in the unfolding process of history, in what has been called temporality, *and* in the creations of culture. There is no preexisting point at which this process of evolution ends. The universal concepts of space and time, which Kant postulated as absolute a priori conditions of all human experience, are no longer conceived of in quite the same way that Kant conceived of them. Space and time, at the present juncture of history, are *signs*, relative to the observer's frame of reference. Cassirer, although a neo-Kantian, ultimately rejects the Kantian a priori conditions for experiencing objective reality as too static. He quotes Lasswitz's criticism of the Kantian position:

Never may critical philosophy presume to define the conditions of experience a priori; it can do so only through the historical process; and just as physical knowledge changes, so, too, will the theory of the transcendental conditions of experience change in the course of history . . . What intellectual instruments will be newly discovered, which ones will vanish from the consciousness of man, is an insoluble problem. It suffices if each cultural epoch becomes conscious of its own intellectual instruments. (Cassirer, 1957, p.471)

Space and time, essential a priori forms in the Kantian philosophy of experience, now, as Cassirer tells us, "sink into the shadows." What the quantum physicist Niels Bohr taught him was

that the general problem of the quantum theory involves a profound failure of the spatiotemporal images by means of which one had previously sought to describe natural phenomena. (p.475)

In Bohr's point of view, we literally do not know which way is up and which way is down. We are suspended, so to speak, in a sea of signs. Space has lost its Kantian status as an absolute form of experience. Time, similarly, is no longer a static form which shapes all experience in the same way. Similarly, the concepts of motion, force, mass, energy, and permanence have no significance apart from a frame of reference. Cassirer observes that in contemporary science, "they only *signify* something; and in general they mean different things for observers who are in motion relative to one another" (p.478).

There is, Cassirer continues, no scientific description of the natural process free from the *subjectivity* of the observer. Physics can never dispense with "the function of concepts and signs." What Cassirer has done is to extend the frame of experience beyond the boundaries that Kant delineated for it. What Cassirer has to give up in exchange for this expanded territory of experience is Kantian *objectivity*. In Cassirer's view, we can have no experience of reality as objective, apart from the subjectivity of the observer. What we have instead of objectivity is reflexivity. For Cassirer, reality is a construction of the web of language, of signs, which man spins out of himself, out of his experience. Cassirer has set the stage for the postmodern conception of reality and for the postmodern conception of the self.

THE SELF AS SIGN

The self, Cassirer says, is a sign, which signifies different things depending upon the frame of reference of the observer. With a new conception of space as a sign, we cannot assume that the self is contained within the skin, any more than we can assume that an atom is strictly a material particle with a definite spatiotemporal location. Just as fields and energy extend beyond the "skin" of an atom, so does the self extend beyond the boundaries of the individual person. This concept of the self allows us to view symptoms not as inherent qualities of an individual, but as signs of a broader social context. A problem or diagnosis is an attribute of a social context or a complex system, rather than an objective attribute of an individual person within that system. When the relations in the larger system shift, the symptoms shift as well. This analogical mode of understanding the self is as ancient as Plato. For Plato maintained in the *Republic* that to understand the individual human being, one must first understand the individual's nature "writ large" in social organizations. The *Republic* is based on this fundamental analogy between the individual and the wider social context of the individual.

The postmodern view of space as a sign allows for an extension of the notion of self beyond the boundaries of the individual to the wider social context. Thus, any member of a family may be the bearer of a symptom, the identified patient, and the role may be passed from one family member to another. The problem is not "in" an individual, who happens to be the bearer of the symptom for purposes of coming to therapy. The problem is in the broader social context or, to use a metaphor from physics, the "field" of that individual.

Peirce, who was ahead of his times in many ways, thought of the self as more like a wave than like a discrete, rigid entity such as a particle. He criticized the psychology that identified the soul with the individual ego: "The ego is a mere wave in the soul, a superficial and small feature . . . the soul may contain several personalities" (1955, p.258). Peirce also remarked upon the self as inseparable from other people in a person's social context:

> . . . the man's circle of society (however widely or narrowly this phrase may be understood), is a sort of loosely compacted person, in some respects of higher rank than the person of an individual organism. (p.258)

One implication of Peirce's semiotic view of the self for therapy is that one cannot merely treat the individual, but must take into account the "circle of society" or social context of that individual as well.

THE SEMIOTIC SELF

Viewing the self as a sign allows for a myriad of perspectives. In a therapy that takes a semiotic point of view, a diagnosis is not an invariant attribute of an individual. Symptoms arise in relations, in contexts. If the relations or contexts are changed in relevant ways, the symptoms change or disappear. Symptoms are ambiguous, fluid, and dependent on the perspective of the observer — including the bearer of the symptom. Two therapists may interview the same patient and come away from the interview with entirely different diagnoses and ideas for treatment.

Peirce tells us that when we think about ourselves, the self is a sign. Peirce (1955) says that a person's thoughts are: "what he is 'saying to himself,' that is, saying to that other self that is just coming into life in the flow of time" (p.258). Our selves are ambiguous signs even to us. Our past is a kind of *bricolage* of signs, which we attempt to construct in the present. This is the paradox of reflexivity, of the self as both agent and object, both "I" and "me." The self of the past is not the same self as the one in the process of coming to be in the present.

We can see how this idea plays out in the process of therapy. As therapy opens up ever new patterns of meaning in our lives, we may come to punctuate sequences of past events differently. We may see certain events as leading up to other events, connecting in our minds two events that previously seemed unconnected. One event may now appear to us as a sign or metaphor of another event. The very reality of past events changes for us as we sift and strain them for meaning in the light of present experience.

Thus our lives appear to us as polysemic texts, filled with many different possible story lines, many different possible sequences of events. The postmodern narrative style does not proceed forward in an uninterrupted chronological temporal flow. Time is not adequately expressed by language that presents events in linear sequences. We give meaning and order to our lives by rearranging the order and sequence of events. "Memory," writes Thomas Sebeok, "is, of course, continually refigured to ensure the maintenance of positive self-esteem" (1991, p.43).

As we have seen, in the postmodern world language has changed its function. The words we use to describe postmodern reality are polysemic images rather than iconic representations of a preexisting real world. What we need is a language of images, of metaphors, to describe a reflected reality. Narratives that are essentially postmodern loop back upon themselves, as the past is continuously reshaped in the present. Signs in the present, like the *petite Madeleine* of Proust's narrator, serve to recover the past and distill patterns of significance from past events. And, as Proust's narrator would have it, the sequences that are discovered or recovered in the reflecting consciousness of the present are in a sense more objective, or at least more significant, than the immediacy with which discrete events were experienced in the past. Reflection, Proust would teach us, is an aspect of experience as real as any other.

A past event no longer appears as simply an objective material reality determining our lives in the present. The past is, rather, an ambiguous sign, a metaphor, indicating different directions that the present self may take. A past event has many different meanings. An incident of sexual abuse, for example, may provide a reason for failure in life, for continuing victimization, or it may provide the means of achieving a higher level of compassion and humanity in the present. A sexually molested child may be seen as a metaphor for a parent, for very often we find that a parent of an abused child has also been a victim of sexual abuse. The daughter's victimization often reflects the mother's.

This way of looking at sexual abuse is not to diminish the horror of the abused child. It is, rather, an attempt to seek out a more profound level of meaning or significance of the child's pain. We all try to find meaning in the suffering and oppression we have endured in life. As Frankl observed (1990), one is free to adapt an *attitude* toward a tragic situation. One may even say that the endeavor to find meaning or positive value in suffering is a natural tendency among human beings. It is an attempt to come to terms with the paradox that we are both determined and free, both objects and agents, both creatures and creators.

IMPLICATIONS FOR THERAPY

A semiotic perspective has important implications for family therapy in the postmodern world. One implication is that the reflecting and creating mind constructs what we perceive as reality. Reality appears to us reflected in a mirror of signs. Another implication of semiosis is that the individual self is inseparable from a wider social context. An individual is an analogy or a metaphor for that social context. Problems of the individual may be seen as analogies or performances of problems in the individual's wider social context. The family therapist generally looks to the client's family context, or at times to the contexts of work or school, to discover the larger problem that is being analogically expressed or performed.

Strategic and systemic family therapy provide the therapist with tools for addressing problems in the family. But in the process of solving the family problem we must ask ourselves if an even wider context must be considered. Is a family problem not a performance of a problem in the larger society, a problem that will continue to seek expression in individual families? In his *Republic*, Plato posed the question of whether one could live as a just person in an unjust society. For an indisputably just and benevolent man like Socrates, who was put to death by the Athenian state, Plato's answer was clearly "no."

Just as in decades past the family therapist was faced with the dilemma of how an individual person could remain healthy in a dysfunctional family, now she is faced with the dilemma of how a family can remain healthy in a larger society that grows ever more dysfunctional. To resolve this dilemma would involve inquiry into issues of race, of gender, and of class, issues that are beyond the scope of this chapter and of this book. But questions about the injustices of society arise from any analogical mode of thinking about the self. And these are questions that must be addressed by family therapy in the future, as it becomes focused on the larger society as the context of the family. In this vein, Madanes (1995) has argued for a "therapy of social action" to address the problems of violence in our society. And social therapists such as Lynn Hoffman (1995) have argued that family therapy, in order to be effective, must become cognizant of the wider social issues of race, gender, culture, and class.

Symptom as Sign: A Case Example

I shall conclude this discussion with a case example in which I view a symptom as a metaphor for a social context or family problem. A fourteen-year-old anorectic girl, Betty, came to therapy with her family. The family previously had sought treatment from another professional, who had been seeing Betty alone in therapy. After six months of individual therapy there had been no improvement and Betty's weight had dropped to the dangerous level of seventy-eight pounds. She was very weak and had frequent bouts of illness, which caused her to miss several weeks of school. Seeing me was a last resort to avoid hospitalization, to which Betty was violently opposed. Betty's parents also wanted to avoid hospitalization, as they did not want her to miss any more school. They also preferred to treat Betty's symptoms without medication if at all possible.

The family asked if I would out of courtesy consult with the other professional, who was very highly regarded in the community. I agreed and phoned him after my first session with Betty's family. During our conversation, the professional referred to Betty as angry, depressed, and uncooperative in therapy. He had recommended an antidepressant medication for her depression and hospitalization because she was continuing to lose weight at a dangerous pace. He was also concerned that Betty's symptoms might be rooted in a past occurrence of sexual abuse by her father. He cited a recent study which showed that fifty percent of outpatient anorectics and seventy-five percent of inpatient anorectics had been sexually abused.

We have here an example in which two professionals perceived Betty in very different ways from differing frames of reference, neither one more "true" than the other. From my perspective, I found it useful to see Betty as benevolently sacrificing herself for her mother, who, it seemed to me, was lonely, isolated, and starved for affection in her marriage. Betty, in my eyes, was bringing her mother to therapy, albeit by the extreme means of self-starvation. In the first session, I asked Betty's mother to "pretend" that she was worried and asked the rest of the family to pretend to help her by comforting her. When Betty recognized that I saw her as sacrificing herself to get help for her mother, her eyes filled with tears. From that point on she was extremely cooperative with me in therapy, throwing herself enthusiastically into games of helping mother with her "pretend" worries. One of the games that Betty and her brother enjoyed most was "pretending to cook." They would prepare a pretend meal for their mother with the toy kitchen utensils and foods in my playroom. Even Betty's father joined in this game when I insisted that the entire family participate.

I did not find evidence of Betty's having been sexually abused, although of course I explored this possibility very carefully. I interviewed Betty alone, making it safe for her to disclose any incidents of her father touching her in ways that made her uncomfortable. Additionally, I saw Betty and her younger brother in a session, again gently exploring the possibility of abuse. In the end, I was satisfied that Betty had not been abused. In the course of family therapy, Betty's father became more attentive to his wife, changed jobs to reduce his stress, and began planning a vacation with his wife. Betty then began to cheer up. She offered to baby-sit for her younger brother so that her parents could go away for a weekend alone. As her parents' relationship improved in therapy, they were able to work together cooperatively to oversee their daughter's eating. In therapy, we agreed upon what were reasonable portions and varieties of food for Betty's meals. Mother and father began to feel more in control as parents, making sure at each meal that Betty ate enough food to gain weight and recover her strength. Betty's father took an active role in helping her catch up with her school work.

Betty soon began to eat more and gain weight. Released from worrying about her mother, Betty spent more time with friends, joined the school chorus, and won the lead role in the chorus musical production. After six months, Betty exceeded the goal weight set by her pediatrician and was behaving in age-appropriate ways. The family and I decided that therapy could be terminated and that I would make follow-ups by telephone. A year later Betty was eating normally and maintaining a healthy weight.

One way of seeing this situation is to view Betty's anorexia as a sign, signifying different things to professionals with differing frames of reference. The "reality" of this client and the symptoms she presents are dependent variables, tied to each therapist's frame of reference, to the way each one constructs the situation, and to the story or hypothesis each therapist creates. Both approaches are potentially capable of resolving Betty's symptoms. I do not ask what is the "true" cause of the anorexia, for truth is not at issue here. Rather, I am concerned with the meaning of the symptom, its significance in the family. The main question is which construction, which story, provides an effective and timely solution to the problem, most in keeping with the goals of Betty and her family.

CHAPTER 4

Constructing Family Values:
Therapy and Fiction

All happy families are alike.

— Leo Tolstoy

THE FAMILY THERAPIST works with madness and pain in families, with problems and unhappiness, with abuse, with violent and life-threatening situations. The therapist can become so involved in human misery that the notion of a happy, healthy family is something she rarely thinks about. Happy, healthy families do not generally come to therapy. Yet the therapist may at times need to have an idea of what a healthy family is, a goal of therapy other than merely the absence of serious problems. "What," we ask ourselves, "does a happy family look like in the postmodern world?" "Are all happy families really alike?" We lack an omniscient narrator like Tolstoy's who can tell us with certainty what a happy family is and what tragic consequences will ensue when certain social norms defining family structure are defied.

Therapists have tended to shy away from defining what a happy or normal family looks like because traditionally the therapist was thought to be a value-free, neutral observer, whereas happiness and normality are value-laden concepts. But, as we have seen in Chapter 2, an observer is not neutral. The subjectivity of the observer is always a part of what is being observed. The object always reflects back the subject. The therapist's frame of reference, including her beliefs, always has an effect on the system she is observing. And values, like theoretical constructs, are part of a frame of reference. A therapist's values always play a role in therapy, whether or not she is conscious of them. And this being the case, it is more useful to be conscious of one's values than not to be conscious of them. To begin to construct *a* picture (but not the only picture) of a happy family in the postmodern era, I would like to tell you the story of a young couple. This couple came to me for help in constructing their own version of a happy family—a version which was, as it turned out, strikingly different from the dominant values of their social milieu.

THE PERFECT COUPLE

Molly and Jeff were the kind of couple that anyone would admire. They were in their early thirties, tall, blond, and sun-tanned. They had shining blue eyes and were attractively dressed in the latest styles. Intelligent and straightforward, they were truly one of the most delightful couples ever to walk into my office. To complete the happy picture, they had an adorable daughter, Allison, who was approaching her second birthday. Both Molly and Jeff had prestigious and interesting jobs in San Francisco. She was an advertising executive in an international communications company, and he was a college professor. Molly earned a very high salary and was the main breadwinner for the family. Jeff, because of his flexible schedule, was the one who dropped off and picked up Allison from the daycare center. Often, when Molly worked late, Jeff fed and bathed Allison. He was the ideal of a modern, liberated father. Apart from her three-month maternity leave, Molly had never stayed home full-time with Allison. The couple had a lovely townhouse in a fashionable district of the city. They shopped at elegant department stores, bicycled in the park on weekends, and radiated wholesomeness and optimism. Molly and Jeff came from a small town in the Midwest, and their families were very proud of their achievements.

But there were problems which brought this couple to therapy. Molly had become increasingly depressed, and had been experiencing severe pain in her lower back, which was interfering with her ability to work. She was in such pain that recently she had to take several weeks off work. Molly and Jeff also had been having arguments more and more frequently, and they were afraid that the constant fighting was becoming damaging to their relationship. Molly's physician advised her to reduce the stress in her life as much as possible and to go to therapy for her depression. And so Molly came to consult me.

MOLLY'S DILEMMA

In our first conversation, the meaning of Molly's depression and her physical pain came to light. Tearfully, she confessed to me how much she wanted to stay home and raise her daughter herself rather than leave Allison with baby-sitters all day. Molly told me how it broke her heart that the baby-sitter was the one to hear Allison's first words and see her first steps. She felt that she was missing out on motherhood. Molly even felt resentful that Jeff had more time with Allison than she did, and she envied their closeness, even though she knew that a loving relationship with Jeff was a good thing for her daughter. Molly often felt angry at Jeff, and their fights were becoming increasingly more heated.

It was not difficult for me to see Molly's back pain as a sign or metaphorical expression of the pain of leaving the baby she adored. The function of the back pain, as I constructed the story, was to enable Molly to stay home with her daughter. Again, I want to emphasize that this hypothesis, this story, does not in any way deny the real physical pain that Molly was experiencing. My hypothesis that the pain was a sign, a metaphor, was simply a useful way to help me go about relieving the pain.

Molly told me that she very much wanted to have another child and stay at home with both children, but she didn't see how she could afford to quit her job. The couple needed her income to survive. And recently there had been budget cuts at the college where Jeff taught. Because he did not have a tenured position his job was not secure. Molly also had a strong desire to raise her children closer to her own parents. She wanted her parents to have time with their grandchildren and vice versa. She longed to move back to the Midwest. Jeff had similar feelings about raising his daughter near his own parents, who lived in the same town as Molly's. And Jeff very candidly admitted that he was beginning to feel resentful about Molly's promotions and raises in salary, as his own tenuous job brought longer hours with no increased pay. He, too, would prefer to live in the Midwest, where the cost of living was not so high and the family could live on his income.

Everyone told Molly that she had a truly enviable style of life. But her lovely home, fashionable clothes, and prestigious job carried with them the price that Molly saw her daughter only two or three hours each day when she felt too exhausted from work and commuting to enjoy her. Molly felt trapped in a situation that others might envy. In fact, her old friends in the Midwest who were staying home with their own children told Molly how much they envied her. In their eyes she was leading an interesting and stimulating life, far superior to the boredom and tedium of staying home. To them she was a sign of modern, liberated womanhood. Molly's intelligence and creativity were so striking that even I wondered if she really wanted to trade her interesting career for the life of a housewife and full-time mother. But in her own eyes, Molly was miserable. She was depressed and unhappy in her present situation. Both Molly and I viewed her "depression" as the result of an external situation and not as an internal fixed attribute. We both believed that the depression would change if Molly changed her situation and was able to spend more time with her daughter.

ALTERNATIVE VALUES

I could see that Molly and Jeff loved one another and were the kind of rare modern couple who valued their marriage and family life above money, career, and prestige. As they began to trust me, they opened up about what they self-consciously called their "old-fashioned" values, which were not the mainstream values of their social milieu. They both wanted Molly to stay home and be a full-time mother, with Jeff becoming the main breadwinner for the family. But they believed that this was an ideal that they could not realize in practice. Realistically, they thought that they could not afford to live anywhere near San Francisco if Molly were to give up her high-paying job. In her profession she was not able to work part-time, which might have been one solution. They could live on Jeff's income with a scaled-down lifestyle only if they moved back to the Midwest or some other place where the cost of living was lower. But they would be giving up Molly's lucrative career, the clothes, the cars, and the lifestyle to which they had become accustomed. Moreover, they would be rejecting the dominant values of the culture, values hard-won by modern women. They felt that nobody among their friends and acquaintances would support a decision to give up all they had, for Molly to stay home. Moreover, each of them was unsure of what the other really wanted. Jeff wondered if Molly really would be content with the modest lifestyle he could provide on his income. Molly wondered if Jeff really would be comfortable living close to his parents, in particular to his domineering father.

"Tell us what to do," they pleaded with me at one session. "We are fighting all the time. Last night after we put Allison to bed, we were too exhausted to go out for food so we had crackers and an orange for dinner. We have no quality time with Allison or with one another." As I considered their request I was concerned that by advising Molly and Jeff what course of action they should take, I would be taking the risk of imposing my own values on them. Often in therapy I have advised couples on a course of action. For example, I would advise parents on the steps they should take in order to get control of a misbehaving child or adolescent. Every therapist who gives directives, and quite arguably even those therapists who do not give directives, is imposing a set of values on a client. Everything about a therapist—the location of her office, her manner of speech, her appearance—conveys the therapist's values and cultural bckground. But giving a directive to help parents get control of a child seems a very different matter from advising a couple to take a 180 degree turn in their life and to adopt a traditional family structure with the wife at home and the husband as breadwinner.

However, I had come to know Jeff and Molly very well during two months of therapy. I was conscious of myself attempting to "read" Jeff and Molly's deepest values, just as an interpreter of a text attempts to penetrate the text's deepest stratum of meaning. When I could "read" this couple's deepest values well enough to know what would make their lives more meaningful, I would be able to advise them on a course of action. Their values concerning raising children seemed to resonate very much with my own, which diverged from the dominant values of most professional women.

But I did not advise staying home to every mother I saw in therapy. In fact, many times, depending on the individual situation, I would advise the opposite. In cases where a husband would lose respect for a wife who left her career to become a homemaker, and where the wife really did not want to stay at home, I would support the wife's decision to keep her job. Another couple I happened to be seeing in therapy at the time, Mark and Elinor, were this kind of couple. Elinor worked full-time, but Mark refused to drop off their daughter at nursery school even though he drove right by the school on his way to work every day. He was pressuring Elinor to quit her job and stay home with their two children. Elinor was afraid, however, that Mark would not help at all with the children if she didn't have a job. Besides, she loved her job and didn't like staying home. Her children were happy and well-adjusted, and did not seem to be suffering from a lack of her attention. After consulting with me a few times, both individually and together with Mark, Elinor decided to keep her job.

But I could see that Jeff's values were different from Mark's. Jeff was the kind of father who wanted to be involved with his children as much as possible from the very beginning. Having contact with his children and being a formative influence on their development from their early years had meaning and importance for him. These were values rooted very deeply in his character. I also realized that Jeff and Molly were immersed in a social milieu of friends and colleagues that made a change of family structure very difficult for them. I think that they had turned to me because they sensed that I might be open to different values than the dominant values of the people around them in the larger culture.

At one point, Molly and Jeff asked me my personal opinion on the subject of young children needing a mother at home. This forced me to reflect upon my own values and the appropriateness of expressing them in a therapy situation. Finally, I decided that it would do no harm to be honest with this couple. I had seen so many parents sacrifice their children's emotional well-being for the sake of material possessions and financial rewards that I felt that I must tell them my thinking on the issue. And so I told Molly and Jeff that I had stayed home with my own children until they were in first grade. And, despite the relative financial hardships to the family, neither I nor my husband had regretted this decision. But I also added that I believed this was a very personal kind of decision that every mother had to make for herself. And every mother would make the decision differently.

REFLECTING ON FAMILY VALUES

Before I would give advice to Molly and Jeff, I gave them a homework assignment for the next therapy session. I asked them both to write down all the negatives of Molly's staying at home and their living solely on Jeff's income. I said the list should be as long as possible and they should work hard at thinking about the negatives. I was not using a paradoxical technique here; I just wanted Molly and Jeff to get a realistic idea of what they might be getting into, so that they would not come to regret their decision later on.

At the next session, they brought a long list. Molly's list included fears of boredom, isolation, and lack of respect by society for a woman who was "merely" a homemaker. She feared criticism by her colleagues and friends. She also feared her family's criticism for giving up a good income and a successful career. Jeff feared the pressure of being the sole wage earner for the family. He was afraid he could not provide the comforts they had grown used to. He was concerned about finding another job. Both were worried about the family tensions they would encounter if they moved closer to their parents. Jeff was afraid of Molly's becoming too enmeshed with her mother, and Molly was concerned that Jeff's domineering father would control their holidays.

For my part, I painted a very gloomy picture of a mother cooped up in the house with a toddler during the long winter months. Molly objected that she would love to spend time making cookies with her daughter and have time to read to her. I told them they would not be able to afford good restaurants or nice clothes. Molly said she would like to have time to cook nice dinners for them rather than rely on fast food at the end of her busy work day. She would sew their clothes.

Slowly, the positives began to outweigh the negatives. Jeff candidly admitted that could not get rid of his deeply rooted belief that the man should be the breadwinner for the family. Finally, it became clear to me that this couple really did want to construct a traditional style of marriage for themselves, so I agreed to help them come up with a strategy to achieve their goal. After some discussion, they decided that Molly would apply for a transfer to the Midwest office of her company. Meanwhile, Jeff would begin looking for a job in the Midwest. They would live on Molly's income until Jeff found a job. Then she would quit her job, stay home with Allison, and hopefully have more children. I suggested that they live at least a two-hour drive from their parents instead of in the same town, so they could keep boundaries around their own little family. We discussed how they could create their own holiday celebrations rather than merely fall into their parents' traditions.

A DIFFICULT TRANSITION

Molly did get a transfer to the Midwest, and the couple prepared to move as soon as the college semester was finished. They asked if they could keep in touch with me by phone, as they felt they might need support through this difficult transition in their lives. I believed that they would not need my support for long, since they probably would have more support for a traditional family structure in the Midwest. I agreed to be available to them by telephone and by letter.

The next year was very difficult for this young family and put a heavy strain on their marriage. Jeff could not find a job, and Molly became more and more frustrated and depressed. They were living temporarily in a crowded apartment, since they wanted to have the flexibility to move wherever Jeff got a job. Molly's work was very stressful, and she was spending as little time with Allison as before. Meanwhile, Jeff was at home full-time with Allison, which made Molly feel angry and resentful and Jeff feel frustrated. As I tried to be encouraging by projecting them into the bright future they had to look forward to, I began to have doubts. Had I advised them correctly? Had I allowed my own values to cloud my vision of what was right for this couple? Had I helped them to make the right choice after all? Only time would tell.

A year and a half after Molly had first consulted me, I received a letter from her. Jeff had finally found a good job and they were looking for a house in the city where he would be working. Molly had quit her job. And best of all, they were expecting another child. They were very happy that they had held out for what they truly wanted in the face of hardship and stressful times. Molly wrote that she felt genuinely fulfilled staying home with her daughter. True, there were difficult times, when the weather was too bad to play outside or when she felt isolated and lonely. She sometimes missed her friends and colleagues in California, and she especially missed the good weather. But she felt much happier with her life now and had been experiencing no depression or back pain. The couple no longer had terrible fights. They felt in love more than ever. Molly thanked me for supporting their choice.

Molly wrote to me again eight months later when their second daughter, Jennifer, was born. Molly was delighted that she was able to stay at home with her new baby. Jeff was doing well at his job and had gotten a promotion. I decided to write to Jeff and Molly to ask if they would collaborate with me in writing their story.

REFLEXIVITY

A few weeks later, I received a ten-page letter from Molly with permission to quote from it. Here are some excerpts from what she wrote.

If we had to do it all over again, I don't think we would change a thing. As difficult as it was, it was definitely a learning experience for both of us. Jeff and I have a better relationship because he understands what it's like to be a stay-at-home "mom." He knows how frustrating it can be, how boring it can be. He's very understanding about what I go through every day. He doesn't expect dinner on the table when he walks in the door, but is thrilled when it is.

Molly reflects upon prevalent social norms, questioning their real value:

There seems to be a prevalent idea that husbands/fathers should be able to do whatever they want after work and on weekends and that they are still a little detached from parenting. And by "parenting" I don't mean just disciplining or feeding but all of the daily jobs like diapering, burping, walking, bathing, rocking, all of the "small" things that make babies and children feel safe, protected, and loved. I know that our girls have flourished with the love and care they get from Jeff.

In the reflecting mirror, things are not what they appear to be. Financial success, prestige, and happiness are all exposed as *signs* — ambiguous, shifting, and ephemeral, their meaning always dependent on the observer's frame of reference.

If we were still in California, both of us would be working full time, both girls would be in daycare, and we'd never see them enough. Jeff just walked in and said that he loved me and he was very happy that we made the decision we did for me to stay home. He hears the women at work talk about their children (in daycare all day) and how uncontrollable they are. Staying at home means getting over the sense of being deprived; being able to see the advantages and rewards of a decision that is keeping the extra money out of reach.

My point here is not to endorse Molly and Jeff's particular
choice of values. These values are not, as I said before, the right
choice for every couple. What *is* important for every young family,
however, is the process of reflecting on values and alternative
forms of family structure before making a decision about what is
right for them. What *is* important is challenging and questioning
dominant values in the light of one's own subjective experience and
what one finds meaningful in life. One asks oneself if a cultural
form, a particular story, truly reflects oneself or if it seems alien
to one's deepest feelings and beliefs. Is this a role in a story
that someone else has created, or is this one's own choice? This
is an attitude of reflexivity, of active creativity toward life, of
playfulness, rather than an attitude of passive compliance, an
acceptance of things as they are. It also requires a great deal of
courage.

A creative approach to life is not, however, without its draw-
backs. For one thing, one does not seem to fit in anywhere in
particular. Molly writes that she does not feel that she "fits in" with
the other mothers in her neighborhood who stay home with their
children, because she had a career and knows that she will return
to it some day. Her interests are different from theirs. Yet she
doesn't seem to fit in with the mothers who work full-time either,
because they don't understand what it is like to stay at home with
their children. In the balance, however, Molly feels that her decision was the best one for her, because it was the one that gave her
life meaning and value. Signs that indicate to her that her decision
was the right one are that she no longer suffers from back pain or
depression.

The postscript that Molly adds to her letter is truly extraordinary
in the way she captures in a simple yet profound event of daily life
the experience of reflexivity at the heart of what is truly creative
and meaningful in human life.

> I just realized that I didn't tell you how much joy I get
> from being at home. I guess I figure that people know, but
> I should tell you that it is the most rewarding thing I've
> ever done. Just the other day I spent an hour on my bed

with Jennifer, face to face, nose to nose, just looking, smiling, talking, watching her watch me. And I saw in her eyes all of the love that I feel for her. I know that's really corny but it's true. Our daughters are so happy, and bubbly, and loving I wouldn't have it any other way.

PLAY AND REFLEXIVITY

It is remarkable and yet unremarkable to me that Molly singled out this particular experience of mother-infant reflexivity as what transformed the drudgery of motherhood into a valuable creative experience for her. In the experience of reflexivity, a mother moves outside of herself and sees herself from the vantage point of her child and vice versa. And the child, seeing herself reflected lovingly in her mother's gaze, begins to form a sense of self, a me, and a me that is loved.

This act of a mother mirroring her infant is what D. W. Winnicott (1971) called *play*, which he viewed as the wellspring of all creative and meaningful experience, the only sort of experience that makes life worth living. Winnicott tells us that play begins when the infant sees himself in his mother's eyes "as in a mirror." This early experience of play opens the realm of what Winnicott calls *transitional phenomena*, an area of experience that must be classified "between the subjective and objective." It is also what Winnicott sees as the realm of culture and cultural experience. This transitional realm is not the experience of permanent objects, nor is it merely an unconnected flux of purely subjective sensations. It is a realm of experience between the factual and the fictional. In the transitional realm, the factual appears fictional and vice versa. It is an area, according to Winnicott, whose central truth is that *paradox* must be accepted. It is, to extend Winnicott's notion, the realm of the mirror. We cannot resolve the question of whether we make the world or find it there. The object bears within it the image of the beholder, just as the the mother's eye reflects the image of the child. And it reflects not merely the beholder as an individual, but as a product of culture. But the beholder is also shaped by the object, as the mother sees herself in her child.

FICTIONS AS CONSTRUCTIONS

Tolstoy's Anna Karenina was one of the first heroines of modernity because she rejected, with tragic consequences, a traditional social role in which she was unhappy. Molly, as we have seen, came to choose the very role of mother, wife, and homemaker that Anna rejected. The difference is that Anna Karenina fell into her role without reflecting on it, whereas Molly was consciously able to relfect on what she wanted and create a plan to make a successful transition. Both Anna and Molly penetrated beyond the appearances of the fixed social roles in which they found themselves, testing these roles against the touchstone of their own experience. Molly's experience revealed to her that having a prestigious career was not as personally satisfying to her as being a full-time mother to her daughters. This motivated her to create her own story of postmodern womanhood.

Comparing the fictional Anna with the real Molly makes us aware of the constructed nature of all social norms and values. Values that appear to be eternal and immutable realities are exposed as human constructions, subject to the changes of time. And in an important sense, social roles and values are fictions. The word "fiction" comes from the Latin word *fictio*, which means a making or counterfeiting. A fiction is something imagined, something not real, as opposed to a *factum* or fact, a thing that has actually happened or is true.

FICTIONS, IDOLS AND REALITIES

In the mirror of signs, the line between *fictio* and *factum*, fiction and fact, becomes blurred. Financial success, prestige, and an interesting career may seem like undeniably positive values to the postmodern woman, factual guarantors of happiness in our society. These values seem too sacred and hard-won to have their reality challenged. But Molly, in challenging them, illuminates their essence as cultural constructions, as signs, and the essence of all social roles as constructions or fictions rather than as hard, permanent facts.

Francis Bacon, a deep-minded philosopher in the seventeenth

century, identified the numerous false realities in human society as "idols of the marketplace." He noticed that signs that referred to merely fictive entities were treated by many people as if they stood for real things. And Bacon went on to say that the human mind must be freed from being deceived by these idols by revising its attitude toward the social world, and learn to perceive correctly the fictive entities created by human beings in their social interactions.

Reflecting on social roles and comparing them with lived experience, including the experience of loving and being loved, reminds us that just as a fiction is a construction, a text, so also are social conventions. Social roles and meanings are fictions in a way similar to the way that the novel *Anna Karenina* is a fiction, in that both are constructions, products of the human mind and not hard, indubitable facts. As we are readers of the fictional *Anna Karenina*, Molly is a reader of social "reality," a reality on which she reflects and which she ultimately rejects.

Here, I suggest, we find the real significance of stories for therapy. As stories are fictions, so also are our lives and the lives of our clients. Phyllis Gorfain (1986), in a discussion of *Hamlet* that continues the theme of reflexivity begun in the earlier papers of the *Semiotica* volume, comments, "The seeming opacity and permanence of social arrangements become refractable in the prism of a fiction" (1986, p.210).

Gorfain's paper makes the point that great literary tragedies like *Hamlet* illuminate the limitations of our social forms and values and force us to extend the boundaries or frame of what is "fictional" and what is "real." *Anna Karenina*, I suggest, is another such text. Consider also Nora in Ibsen's *A Doll's House*. Nora, by reflecting on the unsatisfying role in which she found herself, was ultimately able to step out of that role. Although she considers suicide, Nora, in contrast to her fictional counterparts Anna Karenina and Emma Bovary, rejects it. By her reflexive and liberating act of self scrutiny and reconstruction, Nora becomes the first truly modern heroine. She created a new myth for modern womanhood. Molly, by turning the mirror onto the very role of modern womanhood created by Nora, steps into the postmodern era. The myth that had shaped her life is abandoned in search of a new one that she must create for herself. What Nora and Molly have in common is reflexivity. Each of them ceased to perform for others in a socially approved role and became an audience to herself.

THE THERAPIST'S MIRROR

What changed the course of Molly's life was the process of reflexivity, in which she became both a spectator of culture and an active participant in its creation and evolution. And somehow this process of turning over cultural norms, to see if they reflect something of ourselves, seems more real or more genuine than the impermanence of what it exposes, that is, the prevalent values that the society presents as factual reality. To Molly, the value of being a successful, professional woman who had no time for her children was "fake," not "real." She had tried this role and found that it held no meaning for her. It was also making her physically ill. And Molly had the courage and wisdom, but also the creativity, to pursue her personal vision of what was meaningful.

The family therapist, along with Molly, is both reader and author of new cultural realities. In the process of therapy, social conventions, such as the roles of mothers and fathers in caring for children and the roles of husbands and wives, come under close scrutiny. And in therapy, these roles are exposed as just what they are — conventions, fictions, or even idols, rather than absolute values. Therapy thus becomes a rite of transformation, a liminal place outside of or transcending rigid social structures, where a more meaningful self may be constructed. And this self, as we have seen, is a socially evolving self, a self in the context of experience, a self in production, and not a static entity with rigid, objective structures. And the objectified self, the self that we thought we knew, dissolves into an illusion.

In a somewhat different context, Victor Turner called the transformative process of reflecting upon social roles and values "play." For Turner, it is by playing that new social realities are brought into existence. Play is a *"bricoleur* of frail transient constructions." The process of play, writes Turner (1983), reveals to us "the possibility of changing our goals and, therefore, the restructuring of what our culture states to be reality" (p.234).

Therapy, it would seem, has much in common with play in

Turner's sense of the word. In its endeavor to help families create happier lives, family therapy inevitably comes to reexamine seemingly eternal and God-given "realities," which are actually the prevailing paradigms, or dominant narratives, or idols (as Bacon called them) of a society, crystallized into the appearances of objective reality. By exposing these so-called realities as fictions, as constructions, and confronting them with new, more meaningful realities drawn from a client's own experience, therapy becomes a creative and revitalizing force in the evolution of culture. In this sense therapy has much in common with transformative rituals which, according to Turner, involve a reflexive and liminal stance toward rigid social structures.

PLAYING AND THERAPY

Whereas Turner was interested in play from the point of view of culture and its evolution, Winnicott formulated his own, but overlapping, conception of play from the viewpoint of the development of the individual child. Turner looked at play "writ large" in the novel creations that were the inner dynamic of culture, whereas Winnicott was concerned with play "writ small" in the development of the individual child and the individual adult. Focusing on the creative development of the person, Winnicott (1971) insisted that all genuine therapy is essentially play, a creative activity in which one's assumptions about reality are questioned, overturned, and reconstructed.

> If the therapist cannot play, then he is not suitable for the work. . . . The reason why playing is essential is that it is in playing that the patient is being creative (p.54)

What Winnicott means by being creative is just what we have been discussing here. It is, he says, a "colouring of the whole attitude to external reality." He contrasts creativity and playing with compliance, which he says is a mere fitting-in with the world of objects as one finds it. Compliance carries with it a sense of futility, the absence of meaning. Creativity, on the other hand, is the way in which we find meaning in life, and is, according to Winnicott, a "healthy state of being" (1971). This attitude of creativity, of play, is precisely what allowed Molly to reconstruct her family life into a different shape. And in Molly's account of her interaction with her infant daughter, we see concretely how this aptitude for living creatively is passed on from mother to child. This was Winnicott's view as well, namely, that the "good enough mother" would impart to her baby the aptitude for playing and living creatively.

Play, both writ small in the individual and writ large in culture, involves reflexivity, and vice versa. As Winnicott observed, the child sees himself reflected in the world outside, in his mother's loving gaze, and thereby creates an evolving conception of his own self. Culture, similarly, both finds itself reflected and recreates itself anew in rituals and myths (Babcock, 1980b). It should be clear that play, in the sense that we are using the word here, is not play according to the rigid established rules of a game, such as cards or baseball. It is, rather, play in the sense in which a child plays, ever making up new rules of the game.

Yet another important dimension of play comes to light in this discussion, the dimension of communication. In order to help a client reexamine and reevaluate the system of signs that is cultural reality, both therapist and client must, in a reflexive act, step outside the structures of culture and society. Therapy, in playing with cultural variables, may thus be viewed as a kind of meta-communication, a search for ever new signs to comment upon the system of signs that is culture. It is this aspect of play as meta-communication, of changing the ways in which we classify messages, that Bateson saw as the "essential task of therapy." In another chapter, we will consider more closely Bateson's important notion of the play frame, and the inevitable paradoxes that emerge when therapy moves beyond the everyday realities of common sense and becomes reflexive.

NARRATIVE AND META-NARRATIVE

But now let us return to the question with which this chapter began — the tantalizing question, that is, of happy families, which Tolstoy raised and to which he gave an answer of his own in his novels. Ultimately, in Tolstoy's novels, happiness is never the result of unreflecting conformity, the passive acceptance of what society puts forth as the paradigm of happiness. As the poet Fet observed in a letter to his friend Tolstoy in 1876, *Anna Karenina* puts into question for its readers a society's entire system of values.

> They feel that there is an eye looking at them that is differently formed from their own ordinary purblind eyes. What they consider to be honest, good, desirable, elegant and enviable turns out to be dull, coarse, senseless, and ridiculous. (Tolstoy, 1877/1961, p.xvi)

What happy families, or at least happy individuals, do seem to share in Tolstoy's novels is a reflexive attitude of mind toward the realities put forth by a prevailing social order. By reevaluating society's values from a position to some extent outside the mainstream of society, somewhat liminal characters such as Levin achieve an ability to create, and thereby (paradoxically) to find, meaning in their lives. Thus Levin, at the end of Anna Karenina, reflects:

> but my life, my whole life, independently of anything that may happen to me, every moment of it, is no longer meaningless as it was before, but has an incontestable meaning of goodness, with which I have the power to invest it. (Tolstoy, 1877/1961, p.807)

Levin ultimately finds meaning in family life and in fatherhood, but it is a way of life that he has consciously chosen, a role that he has created for himself. Tolstoy implicitly contrasts the reflective Levin to Anna's brother, Stephan Oblonsky, who inhaled his opinions and values from what was socially in vogue as easily and naturally as he inhaled the smoke from his cigar.

In Tolstoy's fictional narrative, then, we find the peculiarly modern idea that the individual has the capacity to create meaning and purpose in his life, and that this creativity is ultimately the source of happiness. But the world constructed in Tolstoy's narrative is not yet the postmodern world. And we see this by looking beyond the narrative itself to the process of narration. There is always, in Tolstoy, the omniscient narrator external to the events of the unfolding story, who tells us exactly how everything turns out and why it turns out that way. The presentation of time is linear, with only the faintest suggestions of prefiguration in two events of the novel. These are the actual suicide that occurs at the railway station near the beginning of the narrative and Anna's premonitory dream that predicts the manner of her death. But the narrative itself is complete and fully framed. The reader is left only to contemplate with awe the finished creation in all its splendid richness of detail.

For a style of narrative that constructs postmodern reality, on the other hand, we must look to Joyce's *Ulysses* or Woolf's *To the Lighthouse* (to mention only two examples, for there are many), where the signs can never be fully interpreted and there is no external and omniscient narrator who even attempts to interpret them for us. The unfolding of the meaning of the novel is a process that is never fully completed. Each reading, or each "performance," to use Turner's word, creates the novel anew. The reader of the postmodern novel, far from being an objective observer, is inevitably an agent in its creation. The novel emerges in the interaction between the narrative and the reader's mental interaction with it, which in a sense is a part of the narrative as well. The frame of the postmodern novel is extended to include the reader within it, thus constructing a paradoxical reality in which the observer is inseparable from the observed.

CHAPTER 5

Reflexivity, Paradox, and Myth

I HAVE PROPOSED THAT experience in the postmodern world is not experience of objective reality but experience of signs. All of our experience is composed of signs. If we wish to speak of some kind of reality beyond the experience of signs, we must use an analogy such as the classical example of a river into which we cannot step twice, because the river is changing even as we are stepping into it. Or, as the philosopher and literary critic Kenneth Burke has put it, the nonsymbolic realm is the realm of "sheer motion" (1968, p.480). Since signs are inherently ambiguous and may signify any number of objects, experience is ambiguous. To give meaning to our experience, to fix it and make sense of it to ourselves and to others, we express experience by means of other signs, that is, by language. And so the activity of using language to express our experience is inherently reflexive, for it is the activity of using signs to comment upon signs. We form highly complex symbol systems *about* symbol systems and, according to Burke, it is this "reflexive capacity," this second order use of symbols, that is characteristically human (p.24). We may think of these two orders of signs as first and second order systems or, as I think more useful, we may collapse them so as to avoid an infinite regress of signs. The infinite regress, however, seems to appear whenever we attempt to move beyond the confines of the commonplace everyday world, to consider deeper questions of meaning in human life.

Our experience, then, is a conversation with ourselves, a dialogue with our images, both individual and collective, in the mirror of signs. Cassirer (1957) tells us:

> No longer in a merely physical universe, man lives in a symbolic universe. They are the tangled threads which weave the symbolic net, the tangled web of human experience. . . . Language, myth, art and religion are parts of this universe. . . . No longer can man confront reality immediately; He cannot see it, as it were, face to face. . . . Instead of dealing with the things themselves man is in a sense constantly conversing with himself. (p.27)

The reflexive use of signs — that is, the use of signs to comment upon the signs that constitute experience, implies that our formulations of experience will inevitably produce paradox. For, as Russell and Whitehead warned, any class that allows statements about itself will produce paradox. And so we must be prepared to accept paradox in experience that is molded and shaped by systems of signs, such as language, which is in fact all the experience that we have got. Paradox, according to the dictionary definition, means simply "that which is inconsistent with common experience." Paradox occurs when we move beyond the ordinary. The initial paradox is of course that whenever we narrate events, however faithful our renditions, we are also talking obliquely about language. The shadow of the word falls upon the thing.

Poetic language tends to play upon this fact of reflexivity present in all discourse, as in the playful conversation between Beatrice and Benedick in Shakespeare's comedy, *Much Ado about Nothing*. "Sweet Beatrice, wouldst thou come when I called thee?" "Yea, signior, and depart when you bid me." "O, stay but till then!"

"'Then' is spoken; fare you well now." In this brief example, as in many of Shakespeare's plays, language is not merely the medium by which narrative is expressed, but also the very subject of the narrative. This kind of word play, this oblique reference of language to itself, illuminates the reflexive nature of all discourse and the "word-thing" that is the stuff of all narrated experience. In this poetic usage of language, first and second order systems of signs are collapsed into one system.

Illusions, fantasies, dreams, art, religious experience, and myths weave the threads of paradox into the web of experience, making it richer, more complex, and more meaningful. We cannot rip the paradoxical threads out of experience without tearing apart the very fabric of experience itself. The stuff upon which dreams, plays, or poems are made is not different from the stuff upon which the rest of experience is made. The reader may here take issue with this extension of poetic language — the oblique or reflexive use of language to comment upon itself — to realms other than poetic or dramatic art. I reply that this extension, this collapsing of the realms of the poetic and the real, is a necessary and useful one, for it is the ground of the therapeutic use of metaphor and of paradox in therapy.

MYTH AND CULTURE

Some narrative theorists have proposed that the dominant pattern or frame for understanding our life experience is the story or narrative (White & Epston, 1990). I think that the word *myth* is preferable to story, because it takes into account the reflexive and also the cultural aspect of our experience. When we narrate experience we do not merely narrate stories of ourselves as individuals, but as collective and social beings. I am not suggesting that all of our life stories are myths, for clearly they are not, at least from our limited perspective. But myths, I would argue, are the ground of all our stories, in the same sense that play is the ground of any particular game. A myth is more than just a story of an individual. Myths are at their heart collective and reflexive creations. They have a double reflexivity: the reflexivity of language and the reflexivity of culture. Durkheim (Cassirer, 1970) pointed out that the source of myth is not in natural phenomena but in human social relationships. For Durkheim, myths portray persons as collective and social beings, not as objects with qualities analogous to the phenomena of nature. Myths are reflexive metacultural commentaries, or stories that a culture tells itself about itself (Babcock, 1980b). As social and cultural beings, peoples have framed their life experiences as myths, and vice versa. We create our life stories as myths, but it is also the case that cultural myths create our life stories.

According to social scientists in the tradition of Durkheim, myths express how people define themselves as persons in relation to other persons. Cassirer, although he agrees with Durkheim, takes a slightly different perspective on myth, emphasizing its roots in culture rather than society. Cassirer views the origin of myth not in forms of political and social organizations, but in what he sees as a deeper stratum of communal life: ritual and art, which he calls "cultural forms." These primitive forms, he argues, are rooted more in emotion and feeling than in rationality. Thus, Cassirer (1970) tells us that myth is grounded in language, in religious ritual, and in art—that is, in cultural forms that capture the feeling-quality of experience. For experience, as Dewey remarked, is packaged not only in physical qualities such as color and sound, but in feeling qualities as well:

> [T]hings are . . . settled, disturbed, comfortable, annoying, barren, harsh, consoling, splendid, fearful; are such immediately and in their own right and behalf. . . . These traits stand in themselves on precisely the same level as colors, sounds, qualities of contact, taste and smell. (Cassirer, 1970, p.86)

In Cassirer's view, these feeling-qualities are preserved in the mythic stratum of experience. Myths have a feeling-quality about them. A myth may express or convey fear and pity, like the myth of Oedipus in Sophocles' account, or sexual desire, like the myth of Oedipus in Freud's account, or fear of sexuality, like the myth of Oedipus in Woody Allen's account. Myths remind us that stories are experienced not with bland neutrality but with feeling and emotional tone. These feeling-qualities are bound up with the stories we tell of experience, much as a feeling is bound up with the story in a dream. A dream sequence may be frightening or peaceful or anxiety-provoking or something else, but a dream is never neutral. Cassirer calls this the "immediate qualitativeness" of experience. Myths are inherently paradoxical. On the one hand, myths seem to be very real patterns of experience which are repeated through centuries and from which we cannot escape, such as the myth of Oedipus as Freud interpreted it. As Thomas Mann (1937) has remarked, "Life, then—at any rate significant life—was in ancient times the reconstitution of the myth in flesh and blood" (p.35). Myth, Mann continues, is the way in which life finds self-awareness. On the other hand, myths are constructions of art, works of dramatic or narrative fiction. For Freud, the myth of Oedipus embodied universal childhood sexual fantasies that govern all of our relations with others. As Woody Allen similarly (although humorously) suggests in his film *Mighty Aphrodite*, myths do not reside in an Olympian play region, far removed from everyday life. Rather, myths are all around us, although they are not always visible to everyone. Myths intrude with peculiar intensity into our day-to-day lives, and, if we remain blind to them for too long, they may rule our destinies. Tragic characters like Oedipus and Cassandra appear in new guises, reminding us that history repeats itself. What occurred in the Greek plays as tragedy recurs in Allen's film as farce.

NARRATIVE STYLE

To look at the various ways that myths have been interpreted we must look at what Bateson (1972) called the "play frame" and how various narrative styles make use of the play frame. According to Bateson, the play frame distinguishes between levels or classes of messages. It is a meta-message, Bateson tells us, which comments upon and tells us how to take other messages: "A fantasy or a myth may simulate a denotative narrative and to discriminate between these types of discourse people use messages of the frame setting type" (p.190).

This distinction seems to imply that a denotative narrative gets somehow closer to the reality of the event than does the fantasy or the myth. A boundary or frame defines these experiences as less real than the commonsense reality of everyday life, the subject of what he calls "denotative narrative." This is analogous to the way the frame of a painting separates the painting from the wall on which it hangs. The distinctions encompassed by Bateson's distinction of play and not-play are far-reaching. They include dreaming as opposed to waking, fiction as opposed to real life, madness as opposed to sanity, illusion as opposed to reality, religious experiences as opposed to commonsense day-to-day reality, and of course myth as opposed to denotative or historical narrative. The need for a play frame separating the two kinds of narrative, Bateson tells us, "is related to a cultural prejudice for avoiding the paradoxes of abstraction" (1972, p.189).

But having made these distinctions, Bateson (1979) later collapses them. What, he asks, if the message "this is play" becomes reflexive and comments upon itself as playful and not serious? Then, continues Bateson, "the roof blows off and you don't know where you are." This meta-meta-message creates the paradox that the play frame becomes an instance of itself, a member of a class it seeks to define. When this occurs, as Bateson puts it, "the roof blows off" and it is no longer clear that the kinds of experiences that we are accustomed to framing as play are play after all. This reflexive operation raises the possibility that so-called "play" experience may be as real as the rest of experience.

This is precisely what happens when narrative style becomes reflexive. We, the spectators, become included within the frame of the fictional narrative in such a way that we are as fictional as what we are observing. To illustrate this, let us consider two examples of narrative style in film. A nonreflexive form of narrative such as that of Woody Allen keeps the play frame intact. The mythical figures of Oedipus and Cassandra are placed in the unmistakable "play frame" of the film, which is firmly framed off from the lives of the spectators watching the film. Allen preserves the distinction between art and real life. His style of narrative does not frame the spectator within the film. The style does not comment on the play frame and qualify it.

This style of film narrative contrasts with that of, for example,

Milcho Manchevski, the director of *Before the Rain*. This film is an example of a truly postmodern style of narrative in film. Here the spectator is framed right within the narrative, because he must construct the sequences of events and attempt to separate out the strands of illusion and reality. No objective narrator provides a resolution to the puzzles of temporality or of illusion and reality. In the world of *Before the Rain*, where "time is not a circle," past and present, illusion and reality, fantasy and fact, dream and waking are intercrossed and entangled to create a kind of infinite loop, like a snake swallowing its own tail. It is impossible to say where illusion begins and reality ends, where past time stops and present and future time begin. There is a point of intersection between dream reality and waking reality. If we may talk of *mimesis* or imitation with respect to this film, it is a representation of human reality as an ontological knot that loops back upon itself, without beginning and without end. It is *mimesis* of paradoxical reality, and the style of narrative is itself an instance of that reality.

Allen's mode of film narrative, on the other hand, is mimetic and imitative rather than reflexive. There is an objective observer narrating the story for us. From this point of view, myths still seem to be located in the fictional realm of fables, legends, fantasies, and fairy tales—that is, narratives that are framed off as less real than narratives of *real* experience. In this sense, myths are still part of what Bateson called the "play frame."

TRANSITIONAL EXPERIENCE

A semiotic and reflexive perspective provides an alternative mode of classification of what is reality and what is not reality. It accepts the place of the paradoxical in experience, blurring the edges of the play frame by stepping outside both the frames of play and of reality. A semiotic perspective also suggests the possibility of transformation between frames. From this point of view, it is not at all self-evident that myth is less real than historical narrative or that dreams are less real than waking experience. Peirce (1877/1955), for example, insists that experience encompasses "the entire mental product." He argues for the reality of dreams, illusions and fictions in so far as we cannot unthink them as having been dreamed or experienced. Similarly, Peirce argues, the experience of God is as real as any other experience. The touchstone of reality in Peirce's view is *experience*. What is real and what is not real is not so much a question of objectivity or proof, but of experience. Dewey (1916), too, saw the value of the concept of experience because it allowed for "continuities" in life rather than dualisms.

Reflexive thinkers through the ages, like poets, have tended to blur the distinctions set by the play frame by insisting that there is always another and higher level of meta-meta-message that comments upon the play frame. Montaigne, in the sixteenth century, valued a reflexive attitude of mind and argued that there is no sharp and irrevocable distinction between sleeping and waking:

> [T]hose who have compared our life to a dream were perhaps more right than they thought. . . . Sleeping we are awake, and waking asleep . . . [W]hy do we not consider the possibility that our thinking, our acting, may be another sort of dreaming, and our waking another sort of sleep? (1580/1957, p.451)

The ancient sophists, who were reflexive philosophers of their day, used the methods of rhetoric and literary criticism to ponder the ways in which works of fiction and art created not mere imitations but actual reality. The myth of Pygmalion, the sculptor whose statue of a woman comes to life, is a similar reflection on the collapsing of the frame separating divine and human creation. Vico, whom von Glasersfeld (1984) called "the first true constructivist," arrived at the same thought in the eighteenth century and seems to have been frightened by it.

Closer to our own times, Winnicott has argued against the framing of dreams, hallucinations, and other forms of illusory and paradoxical experiences from the rest of life. Winnicott suggests, rather, that paradox is inevitable in experience, and particularly in that sort of experience that is most meaningful and most important in human life. He argues that there is a realm of paradoxical experience between the subjective and the objective; he calls this the *transitional* realm of experience. The central paradox in this kind of experience is that the question of whether we create the world or whether we find it cannot be resolved. We create a world in a way similar to the way a schizophrenic creates a delusion. In this vein, Winnicott (1971) argues that there is no sharp line between ordinary health and full blown schizophrenia. Illusions, too, have a place in experience for Winnicott.

> We can share a respect for illusory experience, and if we wish we may collect together and form a group on the basis of the similarity of our illusory experiences. This is a natural root of grouping among human beings. (p.3)

CULTURE AND EXPERIENCE

Haley has long maintained that the behavior of a person with schizophrenia has to do with a confusion in the organization of the schizophrenic's family, and not with some fundamental difference between the schizophrenic's capacity for experience and that of other people. If the hierarchical organization in the family is corrected, he argues, the schizophrenic's experience and behavior move back into the spectrum of what is usually considered to be normal. This point of view, like Winnicott's blurring of the distinction between the schizophrenic's hallucinations and other forms of transitional experiences, is not typical in Western culture with its rigid play frame. It is, however, an idea that is found in many non-Western points of view. Geertz (1973), for example, provides an example of transitional experience from Balinese culture. The ritual drama of *Rangda-Barong*, he recounts, produces a kind of "mass trance" that blurs what we in the West would consider the play frame and allows the spectator-participant to "cross a threshold into another kind of existence." The mythical figures of Rangda and Barong are, Geertz maintains, genuine realities for the Balinese:

> They are, then, not representations of anything, but presences. And when the villagers go into trance they become—*nadi*—themselves part of the realm in which these

presences exist. To ask, as I once did, a man who has *been*
Rangda whether he thinks she is real is to leave oneself
open to the suspicion of idiocy. (p.118)

Geertz suggests that for the Balinese the play frame is not rigid and
fixed, as it is in the West. There is no "aesthetic distance here
separating actors from audience and placing the depicted events in
an unenterable world of illusion" (p.116). Here what we in the
West may think of as meta-meta-messages distinguishing reality
and myth are collapsed into a single message.

Taking an example from another non-Western perspective on
experience, Haley (1993) has pointed out that in Zen philosophy
there is no psychopathology, there are only transitions.

It is particularly significant that in Zen there is a way of
classifying and dismissing human dilemmas that clinicians
might consider serious psychopathology. In Zen, hallucinations, fantasies, and illusory sensations are called
"makyo." . . . The phenomena that could lead to a diagnosis of psychopathology are assumed, in this view of Zen,
to be a product of a special situation of the person and will
change as that situation changes. That is also the view of a
strategic approach to therapy: such phenomena are a response to a situation and not a character defect or a permanent malady. (pp.129–130)

ILLUSION AND REALITY

Another and somewhat different non-Western point of view on
the play frame may be found in Richard Schechner's analysis of
playing. Schechner is a performance theorist and theater director
whose work was much admired by Victor Turner. In his discussion
of playing and Indian philosophy, Schnecher (1988) gives a fasci-
nating account of the Indian notion of *Maya* as both that which is
created by the mind and thus illusory and also that which is created
by the mind and thus real. Moreover, Schechner argues, what Bateson described as within the frame of play is the prior or privileged
reality in the Indian point of view. Play is *lila*, the sport of the

gods, which creates *Maya,* or illusion. "Maya and lila create, contain and project each other — like a snake swallowing its own tail" (p.7).

In India, Schechner argues, it is the commonsense reality of everyday life — and not dreams, illusions, and myths (the more obvious creations of *Maya-lila*) — that is on the defensive. In Schechner's reading of Indian culture, the experience of working daily life is netted or framed out of play, rather than the other way around. Schechner (1988) thus disagrees with Schutz's prioritizing of realities. Working daily life is "not prior or privileged; it is a culture-bound, time-bound reality" (p.6). For Schechner, playing is the prior or privileged reality, the reality that provides a deeper level of meaning in human life. Playing is the underlying, always-there continuum of experience. "Playing, not 'the world of working in daily life,' is the ground, the matrix birthing all experience's exfoliating multiple realities" (p.6).

MYTHS OF OUR TIME

It would follow from Schechner's twisting of the play frame that ordinary life stories are netted out of play reality, which includes myths. We are back at the point we raised previously, that myth is in its nature paradoxical. From one point of view, myths are play and, when the play frame is collapsed, myths are extremely real. The myth of modern womanhood in Western culture may have been created by Ibsen in his fictional "play," *A Doll's House,* but Nora's story is continuously performed and transformed in the "real" lives of millions of women. Shakespeare's myth of Othello, the jealous husband who murders his wife, is a myth that is frequently played out in our culture, as is Shakespeare's myth of teenage suicide expressed in *Romeo and Juliet.*

But the myths narrated in the tragedies of the Greek dramatists have an even more profound significance for our historical era. Freud saw Sophocles' account of the myth of Oedipus as universally relevant to the lives of his patients and his society. Freud selected the incest and parricide episodes from the Oedipus myth and transformed them into universal desires that were the cause of all neurotic illness. But it is striking and curious that Freud entirely ignored the beginning of the Oedipus story. According to the Greek myth, the infant Oedipus was sent away by his parents to be abandoned to die on a hillside. His father had the ankle of his infant son pierced, so that he might be tethered and left to die on a deserted hillside (thus the name Oedipus, which means "swollen foot"). The infant Oedipus survived only by the intervention of a kindly shepherd, who was perhaps the first protective services worker in Western culture. It was the shepherd who saved the child Oedipus from being murdered by his parents. But Freud, who seemed to need to excuse parents from having any role in their children's problems, omitted the infanticide episode entirely from his retelling of the Oedipus myth. Had he not omitted it, had he seen the plight of Oedipus in the context of his parents' attempted infanticide, perhaps Freud would have become the first family therapist.

The abuse and murder of children are, as every contemporary therapist is aware, events that are especially significant in our own time, even if Freud relegated them to fantasies in his. We cannot ignore the fact that parents sexually abuse and even kill their children, in numbers which would have been unimaginable to Freud and which are still unimaginable even to those of us who, in our daily work, cannot deny them. Dorothy Bloch (1978), a child psychoanalyst in the Freudian tradition, concluded after twenty-five years of practice that infanticide was the central preoccupation of her child patients. She too was struck by Freud's "phenomenal omission" of the infanticide portion of the original Oedipus myth in formulating his theory.

> In Freud's hands this story underwent a dramatic transformation. His theory omitted the murderous act of the parents and focused on the deeds of Oedipus. It treated the murder of his father and the marriage to his mother as universal drives. . . . Had Freud applied the same principle of inevitability to the entire myth, his theory would have established the link between cause and effect; the parents' wish to kill their child would then have been universalized as the inevitable first step in the Oedipus com-

plex and as the precipitating factor in the child's preoccupation with incest and murder. (pp.8–9)

Bloch sees the attempted infanticide of Oedipus as the more significant portion of the myth, and her book, *So the Witch Won't Eat Me,* is based on her re-reading of the Oedipus story. But Bloch does not remove the Freudian blinders altogether in her interpretation of myth. In a manner strikingly similar to Freud's attitude toward the actual occurrences of sexual abuse in the early lives of his clients, Bloch prefers to focus on the *fantasy* or *wish* aspect of infanticide, rather than on its factual occurrence in society. She still prefers to see myth as *internal* to the structure of the psyche rather than as an external event in the world. Thus, Bloch maintains that, although she has found the *wish* for infanticide in many parents who were her patients, "cases of actual infanticide are comparatively rare in our times" (p.10).

Although Bloch still wears Freudian blinders to some extent, her recognition of the theme of child murder or infanticide in the Oedipus myth and in the lives of her clients is an important advance in thinking about the problems of children. Although Bloch is a psychoanalytic therapist, working in a tradition that treats the child as an individual and not as part of a systemic whole, she underscores the extent to which families must be considered in the treatment of children.

Both incest between parent and child and child murder are themes frequently played out in our culture. Whether their actual occurrences were as frequent (although unreported) in Freud's society as in our own I cannot speculate. It must be left to the cultural historian to decide whether Western civilization is regressing into a more primitive stage or if the reporting of such offenses simply has become more widespread and accurate. In any case, I would suggest that other ancient myths of child murder, such as Medea, the mother who murders her children, and Iphigeneia, the daughter who is murdered by her father, and Pentheus, the son murdered by his mother, are beginning to reappear (if indeed they ever disappeared) in the life stories of postmodern culture, closing the gap between the reality of myth and the reality of everyday life. Therapy in our day is becoming more and more the redress of primitive wrongs perpetrated by parents on their children. In my experience, even the most "respectable" families are not immune to acts of incest and violence toward children.

MYTH AND RITUAL

Aristotle argued that dramatic poetry, which in his poetics was essentially the creating of myths, not verses, was more "scientific" and more "serious" than history. The reason for this, he argued, is that poetry portrays general or universal truths, whereas history merely gives particular facts (*Poetics* ch. 8, ff.). For Aristotle, the story or *mythos* constructed by the dramatic poet is not a singular story but a universal plot that occurs over and over again through the ages. And Aristotle gives us a very useful definition of myth for our purposes. He says that a *mythos* is the joining of a name with a plot or sequence of events which evokes an emotion (*Poetics*, ch. 8, ff.). Thus, the name "Oedipus" conveys a certain story or plot, the name "Agamemnon" another plot, and the name "Orestes" yet another. All of these express or evoke in us a strong emotion.

Aristotle's view that myth expresses a kind of truth that is more universal than historical narrative is echoed in the work of the cultural historian Johan Huizinga. Huizinga (1950) argues that myth expresses relationships that cannot be described adequately in a rational or logical way:

> We can safely say, I think, that myth is serious to the degree that poetry is serious. Like everything else that transcends the bounds of logical and deliberate judgment, myth and poetry both move in the play-sphere. This is not to say a *lower* sphere, for it may well be that myth, so playing, can soar to heights of insight beyond the reach of reason. (p.129)

Huizinga argues that myths originally were "sacred play" or "played ritual," from which they developed into drama. In the course of time, "the acting out of a myth-theme grew into the regular performance, with mime and dialogue, of a sequence of events constituting a story with a plot" (p.144).

If Turner (1986) was correct in his speculation that drama is rooted in *redressive* ritual, then myths would seem to portray the types of wrongs or crimes that were originally the subject of redress in the culture. Thus, the Greek tragedies presenting the myths of Oedipus, Medea, Agamemnon, and so forth, would be performances of the sorts of misdeeds that were originally the subject of redressive rituals. Myths of incest and infanticide, far from being removed from everyday life in some Olympian play realm, may thus be seen as narratives of actual and widespread events in the culture. Originally these kinds of events were subject to redressive rituals; today, they are the subjects that we must deal with in the therapy room. This connection between redressive ritual and therapy will be further explored in Chapter 7 on the reparation of sexual abuse by means of a therapeutic procedure that has elements in common with redressive ritual.

PLAY AND PARADOX IN THERAPY

Winnicott (1971) maintained that all genuine therapy is essentially play, a creative activity in which therapist and patient together question assumptions about reality. Winnicott was a pediatrician and a psychotherapist in the psychoanalytic tradition, but his ideas about play overlap with some of the presuppositions of strategic therapy. For Winnicott,

> Psychotherapy takes place in the overlap of two areas of playing, that of the therapist and that of the patient. Psychotherapy has to do with two people playing together. (p.39)

Paradox, too, had a central place in Winicott's type of therapy, as it does in strategic therapy and quite possibly in all therapy. Bateson (Jackson, 1968) thought that the essence of therapy was the manipulation of frames or rules of communication. Therapy, in Bateson's account, explores "the ambiguous lines between the literal and the metaphoric, or reality and fantasy." Haley (1990) writes in a similar vein that therapy is serious play, a kind of "game in which the participants maneuver one another" (p.87). Strategic therapy uses "pretend" games and paradoxical strategies that seem to be merely playful. But these playful and paradoxical techniques are based on serious consideration of the multiple levels of communication in the therapy situation, on the meta-meta-messages that qualify the play frame. The games of therapy may be viewed as games of language, that is, games about the way that language is used.

Perhaps the most striking and peculiar game encountered in therapy is that many people come to therapy apparently seeking help to change their lives, and yet they have a stronger need not to allow the therapist to help them. It is as though they are playing a meta-game to the game of seeking help in therapy. Their meta-game is a game of defeating the therapist. Almost a century ago, Freud noticed this kind of meta-game (although he did not use the language of games to describe it) in his patients. Freud (1900) observed that many of the patients who consulted him for help had a stronger need to rebel against his help and prove him wrong. In fact, Freud identified an entire class of dreams that this kind of patient would dream up precisely in order to disprove and discredit his theory of dreams. He called these paradoxical dreams "counter-wish dreams." His patients reported these dreams to him with the motive, he believed, of disproving his theory that dreams were fulfillments of wishes (p.157). Freud thought that the desire to prove the therapist wrong appeared not only in people's dreams but in other aspects of their lives as well. This desire was so widespread, in fact, that Freud expected it not only from his patients but also from the readers of his book, *The Interpretation of Dreams*.

> I can count almost certainly on provoking [a counter-wish dream] after I have explained to a patient for the first time my theory that dreams are fulfillments of wishes. Indeed, it is to be expected that the same thing will happen to some of the readers of the present book: they will be quite ready to have their wishes frustrated in a dream if only their wish that I may be wrong may be fulfilled. (pp.157–158)

BENEVOLENT PARADOXES

One way the therapist can use a client's game of disproving and discrediting the value of the very method he is using to help the client is by the use of paradox. He must move beyond the client's meta-game to a meta-meta-game, which allows the client to change his game. Bateson (Bateson, Jackson, Haley & Weakland, in Jackson, 1968) originally called this technique a "therapeutic double bind." In the rest of this chapter I shall give some case illustrations of the therapeutic use of paradox and the related technique of the "positive connotation" of the symptom in therapy.

Milton Erickson (Haley, 1986) was a master of benevolent paradoxical techniques in therapy. In one case, for example, a young woman consulted Erickson for help in solving a sexual problem. She and her husband had been married for nine months, but the marriage had not been consummated because she would panic at night when they were in bed and persuade her husband not to have sex with her. After trying a straightforward approach and failing to help the woman, Erickson concluded:

> The procedure employed in the first interview was obviously wrong. It was beautifully utilized by the patient to punish and frustrate me for incompetence. (p.156)

Erickson then tried a paradoxical approach with the woman, which turned out to be more successful. He induced a trance and explained to the woman that a consummation of her marriage must occur within the next ten days, although she herself could decide when.

> I told her that it could be on that Saturday night or Sunday, although I preferred Friday night; or it could be on Monday or Tuesday night, although Friday was the preferred night. (p.155)

Erickson continued to state his preference that the woman have sexual relations with her husband on Friday night until she began to show annoyance. Then Erickson saw her husband separately and told him to make no advances to her. The following Friday, the husband reported:

> She told me to tell you what happened last night. It happened so quick I never had a chance. She practically raped me. And she woke me up before midnight to do it again. Then this morning she was laughing, and when I asked her why, she told me to tell you that it wasn't Friday. (p.156)

Erickson then explains the rationale for this strategy.

> The emphasis on my preference posed a most compelling emotional problem for her: since all the days of the week had been named, the passage of each day brought her closer and closer to the unacceptable day of my preference. Hence, by Thursday, only that day and Friday remained. . . . Therefore consummation had to occur either on Thursday by her choice or on Friday through my choice. (p.156)

I had a case very similar to this one, although at the time I had not yet read Erickson's case. A woman consulted me because she experienced severe anxiety and panic attacks whenever her husband made sexual overtures to her. She had been married to her husband for twelve years, and until a few years earlier they had enjoyed normal sexual relations. When she began having panic attacks, she consulted a therapist, with whom she remained in individual therapy for over a year. But in spite of weekly therapy sessions, the woman's anxiety and panic attacks continued and even became worse. This woman finally decided that perhaps a family therapist might help her solve the problem, as she was at her wit's end and was thinking of leaving her husband, even though she was afraid that this would be damaging to their children.

The woman told me that she thought that she loved her husband, although she felt that he was too controlling of her. For example, her husband was the one who always chose the places where they would take their vacations, although she could scarcely object to his choices because they were usually very nice. Her last anxiety attack had occurred when she and her husband were on vacation in a very romantic place in Italy. Whenever her husband initiated sex, she would begin to feel anxious, her heart would race, and she would have difficulty breathing. One evening the attack had been so severe that her husband had to call the hotel physician, who gave her medication to calm her. So, despite the romantic surroundings, she and her husband had not made love on the vacation.

The woman said that she loved her husband and wanted to remain married to him, but she felt no desire to have sexual relations. She also told me that her husband's preference was to have sex on Monday, Wednesday, and Friday evenings. He was a very orderly man, and these days fit in well with his schedule. She, on the other hand, thought of herself as a very spontaneous person. I asked her what sort of things her husband did for her when she had the panic attacks. She said that he held her hand, rubbed her back, and sat with her until she became calm. I asked her to pretend, right there in the session, that she was having a panic attack so I could see what it was like for her. After she did this, I told her to pretend to have a panic attack at least once a day for the next two weeks. [2] She was not to tell her husband whether she was pretending or having a real attack but she should behave the same in either case. If her husband were at work, she should call him and ask him to come home to help her get over the attack. Since his office was only a short distance from their home, she thought that this was feasible for her to ask. I told her that if she felt like it, she could initiate sex during these times or she could just enjoy her husband's affection. We made an appointment for two weeks later. I also asked that her husband come in for a session with me.

At the session with her husband, I explained to him that, following my instructions, his wife would sometimes pretend to have a panic attack but he must respond in the same way as he would if she were having a real attack because he would not know if it were real or pretend. I also explained to him that he must have a lot of patience with his wife and not be too demanding of her until she got over the attacks. Believing the attacks were a medical problem,

---

[2]Barbara Peeks suggested that I use Madanes' "pretend" strategy in this case.

he agreed to refrain from making overtures to his wife until her health improved.

At the next session the woman told me that the anxiety and panic "felt a little different" to her, and she felt like she had more control over the real attacks. She had even initiated sex with her husband one afternoon, although he was unwilling because he felt the pressure of having to get back to work. I told her to continue the pretends for two more weeks and to continue to initiate sex at times when her husband would find it inconvenient. At all costs, she should avoid Mondays, Wednesdays, and Fridays. She should even go to her husband's work and call him away from a meeting and ask him to make love. [3] She should accompany him to a conference he was going to the following week and call him away from meetings to make love.

The rationale here was that since the woman and her husband had experienced good sexual relations in the past, they could do so again if the relations could be on her terms rather than his and if he were to become less rigid. This turned out to be the case. At the next session, she reported that she had had no real panic attacks during the past two weeks, even though she and her husband had made love. She said she felt much better about him. She continued the pretends for another month, but had no further real panic attacks. She also continued to make overtures to her husband at times that were inconvenient for him. Her husband became less demanding sexually but was more content, since his wife seemed to have gotten over the medical problem and had begun to initiate sex.

Haley (1990) observed that the structure of therapy is a "peculiar mixture of play and dead seriousness." The therapist has to decide, and decide fairly quickly, whether a person who consults her is really asking for help or is primarily playing the game of defeating and frustrating the therapist (thereby qualifying his original message by a meta-message), even as he is asking the therapist for help. A useful way of sorting out these two kinds of messages is found in Bateson's theory of symmetrical and complementary relationships. [4]

---

[3] Cloé Madanes suggested this strategy.
[4] Paul Watzlawick (1995) has given a lucid presentation of Bateson's distinction.

THE STRATEGY OF POSITIVE CONNOTATION

Bateson divided relationships into two kinds: symmetrical and complementary. In a symmetrical relationship, two people (or two entities) take a position of equal strength. In a complementary relationship, one person is in a higher position than the other. Bateson noticed that, in play, two dogs starting from a position of symmetry will fight to establish a relationship of complementarity. The play will get increasingly aggressive until one dog lies down and offers his throat to the other dog. This is analogous to what the therapist does when a client attempts to impose a relationship of symmetry on the therapist. The therapist takes a one-down position. This strategic move has been called the "positive connotation" of the client's symptom. The therapist in effect gives the client the message that the symptom serves a positive function in the client's life and should not therefore be changed. The following case example illustrates this strategy.

A young woman was referred to me by her physician because she wanted to lose weight. This woman was unmarried and very lonely, and she felt that losing weight might make her more attractive to men. Although she met many men at the hospital where she worked as a social worker, she was never asked to go out on dates. She had a long history of being overweight, going back to when she was about twelve years old. At the time she consulted me, she and her physician had agreed that she should ideally lose seventy pounds, for her health as much as for her appearance. She had previously been in therapy for six months with another therapist for the same problem but had not been successful at losing weight.

This woman was very pretty and bright and seemed to be motivated to lose weight. I suggested diets to her that had been effective for other clients. I helped her work out daily routines for exercise that were practical and appealing to her. She joined a health club in her neighborhood. After spending each therapy session earnestly devising ways to lose weight, she would go home and do none of the things we had talked about in therapy. Of course, she did not lose a pound. But in our sessions, she would tearfully tell me how miserable, unattractive, and lonely she felt.

After several weeks, I began to notice how frustrated and ineffectual I was feeling about helping this woman. So one day I told her very candidly that despite my best efforts I felt that I was ineffective at helping her lose weight. The problem had defeated me. I also suggested that perhaps she was not yet ready to lose weight at this time, because the idea of being more attractive to men might be intolerable to her. Here I was suggesting that the symptom had a positive meaning or connotation for her. To this she protested that this was not so, that she wanted very much to meet a man. But I insisted that her weight had the positive function of keeping her safe from men. Finally, I asked her if there were any other problem in her life that I could help her with in the remaining minutes of the session, because I was obviously ineffective with the weight problem no matter how hard I tried. To this she replied that she was having difficulty writing her doctoral dissertation — could I help her with the writing block? I said that a writing block was a very serious problem, even more serious than a weight problem, and I wondered if I could really help her. She said she would like to try to work with me on the writing problem anyway, even though I had failed with the weight problem. Finally, I agreed to this, and in the following sessions that is what we worked on.

In the course of the next eight months, she signed up for a diet and exercise program at her health club, one which I hadn't suggested or even known about, and lost seventy pounds. However, she made very little progress on her dissertation, although we worked on this in therapy. Finally, she met a young man who was very attracted to her; after dating for a few months, they became engaged. She was very happy in her new relationship and no longer cared about writing her dissertation. We decided that therapy should be terminated, since it wasn't helping her to write. Eventually, she married the young man. Recently, I received a note from her in which she told me that she had completed her dissertation and received her doctorate.

Coming to therapy placed this woman in a paradoxical situation. She wanted to lose weight, but she did not want to feel controlled by me. Thus, her message "I want your help in losing weight" was qualified by another message "I want to defeat you." By saying that I was ineffective at helping her solve the weight problem, I was giving up control over her eating and admitting defeat. I was also restraining her from losing weight by indicating that she was not yet ready to look attractive. Having proved me ineffective at controlling her, she could prove herself more effective than I was, and prove me wrong, first by losing weight and then by writing her dissertation without my help. By being aware of the different levels of communication and of the paradox that this client both wanted my help and was rejecting it, I could construct a situation in which she could both rebel against me and defeat me, but also achieve her goal of losing weight and becoming more attractive. Or, to put it another way, I changed the game she played by taking a position "meta" to her game.

GAMES AND META-GAMES

Clients who are extremely resistant to the therapist's help even as they seek it out were, as I have already mentioned, well-known to Freud almost a century ago. His method of helping these people was to make them aware of their resistance through interpretations. In Freud's construction of therapeutic reality, a patient's insight into the childhood origins of his resistance was curative. In a strategic approach, on the other hand, the goal of therapy is not insight but a change in the therapist-client interaction, which involves reflexivity. In response to the client's game of defeating the therapist, the therapist arranges a kind of meta-game or a game with new rules in which the client is helped by the therapist in spite of himself. The therapist introduces a second-order reality in order to produce a change that cannot be generated from within the client's frame of reality.

ETHICAL ISSUES

The question arises as to whether this use of meta-games in therapy is ethical, because the client is not aware at the time of what the therapist is doing in the interaction. Is the therapist using meta-games of paradox or positive connotation being "tricky" or "manipulative" because she is not playing by the usual rules of therapy? According to the usual rules of therapy in our culture, a client consults a therapist in a straightforward way and asks for help, and the therapist offers help in an equally straightforward way.

There are several factors involved in answering the question of ethics. First, and most important, there is the issue of the therapist's benevolence. A benevolent and ethical therapist is committed to using all of her skills and experience to help a client solve the problem for which he is consulting the therapist, a problem which is causing him a great deal of pain and misery or else he would not be seeking therapy. It is the very nature of the game that the client is playing that has brought him to therapy in the first place. For a resistant client seeks to defeat and undermine other people in his life, just as he seeks to defeat and frustrate the therapist.

Victor Frankl, an exceptionally humane and compassionate person, was the first therapist to introduce paradoxical interventions into the family therapy literature. The benevolent and ethical therapist, like the benevolent and ethical physician, is concerned with relieving pain and suffering. But no one would expect a physician to explain each and every detail of a medical procedure or each and every detail of why he prescribes one medication and not another. Analogously, how could one expect a therapist to explain every detail of what goes into resolving a client's problem? What does seem to be unethical is for a therapist to continue to see a client for months and even years without resolving the problem for which the client came to therapy.

A client who is resistant to change in therapy is in a sense divided within himself. One part of the self wants help to relieve his suffering, while another wants to resist anyone's help because it feels like control from outside. The ethical question then becomes: "With which of the client's selves should the therapist form an alliance?" Since the therapist's job is to relieve suffering, clearly the therapist must respect more highly that part of the client's self that seeks relief for his own or his family's suffering. Thus, it seems ethically correct for the therapist to bypass that aspect of the client's self that resists change and would keep him in a state of misery for the satisfaction of feeling in control of the situation. Ultimately, the client is in control of the therapy situation because he can leave therapy at any time. It is the part of him that wants to change, to become happier, that keeps him in therapy.

Along with the issue of the therapist's benevolence in using paradox, there is also the issue of the therapist's level of skill. The
strategies of paradox and positive connotation of symptoms should
be used only by the skilled therapist who has had many years of
supervision and experience with these kinds of interventions. They
are not for the inexperienced therapist, for, like any powerful in-
strument in the wrong hands, they may do harm. As Madanes
observes (1995), the therapist should never use paradox simply
because she wants to be original or clever. Paradox, then, should
only be used when it is in the best interests of the client, when direct
methods have failed to resolve a serious problem, and when the
therapist is unquestionably benevolent and not self-seeking.

CHAPTER 6

Reciprocal Sequences:
The String Eater

A SYMPTOM, AS WE HAVE SEEN, may be viewed as a metaphorical communication in a family system.[5] In order to change a symptomatic behavior, I form a hypothesis or create a story about the metaphorical meaning of the symptom and the function of the symptom in the family. This way of thinking helps me to devise an effective strategy or combination of strategies to change the symptomatic behavior. I also think in terms of what I call "metaphorical reciprocity" between sequences in systems. That is to say, one sequence may reflect another sequence for which it is a metaphor. The connection between the two sequences may be thought of as reciprocal, or mutually interactive. A son's misbehavior at school may, for example, signify his father's having problems at work. A girl who

---

[5] I would like to thank Barbara Barbara Peeks for reading and editing an earlier draft of this chapter.

feels lonely and has no friends may signify her mother's social isolation.

Reciprocal sequences occur in systems of social interaction other than families. Haley pointed out that there is a reciprocal relation between the therapist-supervisor system and the family system with which the therapist is working. The hierarchical relationship between supervisor and therapist is reflected or paralleled in the hierarchical relationships in the family the therapist is seeing. Hierarchy is only one of the kinds of sequences that repeat in social systems.

FINDING STRATEGIES FOR CHANGE

When the therapist looks for reciprocal sequences in families, he can change one sequence of behavior, which the patient presents as compulsive and inaccessible to change, by changing a related sequence that is admittedly under voluntary control. In the case I am going to discuss here, a compulsive and dangerous behavior was changed by altering a reciprocal sequence of interaction that was painful to change but admittedly under voluntary control. In this case example, I used three strategies to change the symptomatic behavior. Reconciling and reuniting the extended family was the strategy that finally stopped the client's symptoms. In families where there is long-standing, unspoken resentment, and where family members live at great distances from one another, reuniting a family presents the therapist with a difficult and lengthy task. In this kind of case, the therapist needs strategies to stop the dangerous symptomatic behavior in the short term. In this case I used an ordeal (Haley, 1984) and symptom substitution (Madanes, 1981, 1984) to stop the symptom until the family reconciliation could take place.

THE STRING EATER

A 34-year-old woman, Anne, was referred to therapy because she compulsively ate pieces of string. This habit led to acute abdominal pain, nausea, and bowel problems. Three years previously, in the course of surgery for abdominal pain, Anne's surgeon found a clump of string in her intestines. At a recent visit to her doctor for abdominal cramps, X-rays again indicated an accumulation of string in Anne's intestines. Anne told the doctor that she ate string almost every day. The doctor warned Anne of the medical complications of this behavior, mentioning cancer. When Anne said she felt incapable of stopping on her own, the doctor referred Anne to therapy.

Anne was an attractive, petite woman with long black hair and dark eyes. Originally from South America, she had lived in this country for many years. In the initial session, she summarized the history of the problem. The first thing she thought of each morning when she woke up was eating string. She kept secret caches of string in her room and in her car. She could not resist picking up and eating bits of string when she saw them on the sidewalk. Sometimes she connected pieces of string together in a chain and pulled them out of her throat before swallowing them.

Anne felt that string was a source of low calorie "roughage" helpful to her dieting. She was always trying to keep her weight down, as she feared becoming obese like her mother. She told me that her mother now weighed over two hundred pounds. Although Anne was a very attractive and petite woman, she said that she felt like she was overweight. Because she knew that string was not good for her body, she sometimes would substitute sandwiches for the string. When she ate a sandwich, she told me, she would swallow it in huge gulps, feeling it catch in her throat. She felt like she was trying to "choke down" something, but she was not sure what it was.

Anne said that she had first begun to eat string when she was about twelve years old. She did not remember why she started but thought it might have had something to do with dieting. She also remembered chewing bits of string that she found in her father's workshop in the basement of her house. Anne's father was away on business trips much of the time, and she would play in his workshop, which reminded her of him. At the time Anne began eating string, her parents had been unhappy and bickered much of the time when her father was at home.

Anne ate string for about a year when she was in junior high school; then she stopped. She had no memory of why she began or why she stopped. During Anne's adolescence her father drank heavily and her mother was depressed.

When Anne graduated high school, she left home, completed college, and married a young man she met there, Samuel. This caused disruption in both families because Anne and Samuel came from different religious and cultural backgrounds. Samuel was Jewish and Anne was Catholic. The young couple decided to marry anyway, although both of their families refused to attend their wedding. Anne said that in her marriage she seemed to have everything she had always wanted — financial security, four beautiful children, a lovely home, and a stable relationship. She felt that Samuel resembled her father in his need to dominate his wife. Although he was controlling, he had never been abusive to her. But Anne was terrified that she would end up depressed and obese like her own mother. She felt like she had very little control over her life.

Anne told me that her mother ate compulsively and was now dangerously obese; her physician had advised her to lose weight for her health. Anne was very worried about her mother and wanted to help her find a therapist, but she felt powerless because of the geographical distance between them. She discussed with me the possibility of bringing her mother to a therapy session herself. But this was a remote possibility because her parents still lived in South America.

Anne had started to eat string again some six years previously after her husband had a violent argument with her father. This happened while Anne's father was visiting them during a business trip to the United States. Apparently the two men argued about a trivial matter, but Samuel had lost his temper and yelled at Anne's father. Anne was not present during the incident and did not know exactly what had happened. From that time on, Anne kept secret stashes of pieces of string and ate them, especially after telephone contact with her parents.

Shortly after the incident with Anne's husband and father, Anne's father had referred to her husband's religion in an insulting way in the presence of one of Anne's friends, who still lived in the same town as her parents. From the day he heard about the insult, Anne's husband refused to have anything to do with her father. Anne was effectively cut off from contact with her parents, having only occasional phone conversations with her mother. One of her children had never seen his grandparents. She did not want to hurt her husband's feelings by bringing up the subject of her parents, because the issue was such a painful one between them. She was always fearful that her parents would telephone and her husband would answer the phone, so she kept contact to a minimum. She had seen her mother only once in five years, at her brother's wedding. At the wedding, Anne's uncle told her that her parents were hurting about the breach, and urged Anne to do something to resolve the matter. But Anne felt helpless in the situation. She felt as though she had no power to change her husband's rigid position.

The Symptom as Metaphor

My hypothesis was that Anne's symptom was an attempt to resolve the problematic situation in which she was cut off from contact with her mother. The symptom could also be seen as a metaphor with more than one referent, a multivocal sign. Anne's symptomatic behavior could be seen as metaphorical of her mother, who "stuffed herself" with food to stifle her depression. The connected chains of string could refer to the function of reconnecting Anne with her parents. The string may refer to her father, in whose workshop she had played and devoured bits of string when he was away from home and she missed him.

When I suggested that eating string was connected in some way to the rift with her parents, Anne immediately agreed. She felt that she had to stuff down the feelings of wanting to see her parents. She felt that she had to kill her feelings for her family. But in killing her affection for her parents she felt that she was killing a part of herself. Anne summed it up when she said, "I feel like I am killing myself inside." She recalled that, when she was in the hospital a few years ago, she would have the fantasy that her husband, her children, and her parents would be gathered together around her deathbed in mourning. Here Anne divulged, in metaphor, the function of her unusual symptom: her illness or even death resulting from eating string would finally reunite her parents with her husband, her children, and herself.

Since my immediate concern was to modify the dangerous behavior, I directed that if Anne felt a compulsion to eat a piece of string, she must first cut it into twenty-five pieces. My thinking was that this "ordeal" would be more trouble than eating the string was worth. But Anne objected that she could not cut up a piece of string if she had the desire to eat one in her car. I insisted that she not eat any string unless she cut it into twenty-five pieces; she would have to wait until she got home if she could not cut up the string in her car. Or she could carry a pair of scissors with her. Anne agreed to do this. Further, I directed a substitute for the symptomatic behavior, one that Anne had already discovered herself. If Anne felt the desire to eat string, she was to eat a sandwich, with plenty of lettuce and crunchy vegetables in it. She was to carry sandwiches with her in her purse so she could substitute these when she felt the desire to eat string. Anne protested that sandwiches were fattening, so we had a long discussion about which sandwiches had the least calories. Finally, she agreed to try sandwiches as a substitute for string.

SECOND SESSION

In the second session, Anne reported that she was beginning to feel a connection between her eating string and the need to choke down painful feelings about the breach with her parents. She had not eaten any string that week but had eaten many sandwiches. The urge to eat string was strongest in the late afternoons when she had to help the children with homework, prepare dinner, and put the children to bed by herself while her husband was still at work.

Anne said that the string eating was the only thing in her life that she had not shared with her husband, although he probably suspected, since the surgeon had mentioned string. I observed that quite possibly eating string was the only thing over which Anne felt like she had any control in her life. Anne agreed with this. She and I began to talk about other ways that she could get control of her life, such as taking a trip to see her parents. Anne said she would like to visit her mother, as she often worried about her. But Anne did not want to visit her parents without her husband's blessing, because she did not want to hurt his feelings. I offered to help Anne plan a visit to her parents since it was very important to reconnect with her mother, and we made an appointment for Anne and her husband to come to therapy together.

THIRD SESSION: THE COUPLE

By the time Anne and Samuel came to see me, she already had told him about eating string. She announced that she was so nervous about the session that she had eaten a long piece of string, after having cut it up carefully. I asked Anne to tell her husband what was troubling her and what he could do. Tearfully, she told him that his conflict with her family was tearing her apart. She wanted her parents, her husband, and her children to be all together, just one time. Her husband said he was immovable on the point of seeing her father. He told Anne that she had his blessing to fly to their hometown and visit her mother any time she wished, but he would never see her parents. He was too hurt by her father's insulting his religious beliefs. Anne tearfully asked her husband if he would even go to her mother's funeral if she were to die. Her husband said he would not attend her funeral if Anne's father were present. He would never agree to be in the same room as her father.

Anne sobbed at hearing this. She blurted out that the only way she could visualize her husband and her parents in a room together was at her deathbed. Her husband said that even if she were dying he would not be in the same room as her father. I reassured Anne that she would not have to go to this length. However, this breach between her husband and her parents was a very serious problem. Anne repeated that her one wish was to have everyone be together just one time. Her husband only had to be civil to her father. He said no, never would he bend. He would never see her father and she could just keep eating string if she had to.

THE RABBI'S STRATEGY

I hypothesized that the family had to be reorganized in order to stop Anne's self-destructive behavior. Somehow, the rift between

Anne's father and her husband had to be healed, so that Anne could see her parents. Even the children were becoming affected by the tension between their parents and grandparents. One of the girls had recently been hospitalized for acute abdominal pain, for which a medical cause could not be found.

Reuniting the family presented a challenging task, given the terrible nature of the insult to Anne's husband. I knew that I was going to have to be creative in finding a way to persuade Samuel to forgive his father-in-law. Knowing that Samuel was devout, I decided to consult a Rabbi to get ideas for formulating a strategy that would move Samuel to forgive his father-in-law to save his wife's health. The Rabbi told me two relevant points of Jewish law. First, a husband has a solemn duty to do everything he can to preserve his wife's physical health. Second, the content of the Yom Kippur (Day of Atonement) liturgy requires a Jew to forgive another person no matter how seriously he has been wronged. If he held in the resentment and refused to forgive, the sin would hurt his own soul.

I used the Rabbi's information to devise a strategy for the daunting task of reconciling Anne's husband and father. First I met with Samuel alone to establish trust. In this session I disclosed that I too was Jewish and had experienced religious prejudice, which had been very painful. I also expressed my concern for the seriousness of his wife's symptom and a concern that the children would also be affected. Samuel told me that he also was worried about his wife, as he could see that she was unhappy. I asked him to accompany his wife to the next session.

In the following session with Anne and Samuel I initiated a discussion of religious observance. Samuel and Anne said they were very devout Jews. I observed that no doubt Samuel would be familiar with the Yom Kippur liturgy, which said it was a sin for a Jew to hold anger and resentment in his heart and not to forgive. It was a sin because it hurt a Jew's own soul. Even though the insult was truly horrible and seemed unforgivable, Jewish law required forgiveness even for this.

Samuel became very upset at hearing this. He said he knew this to be so, but he could not change his mind regarding Anne's father. I looked him straight in the eyes and repeated that not to forgive if forgiveness were asked was a sin upon Samuel's soul. Moreover,

Samuel had a duty to preserve the physical health of his wife. At this, Samuel burst out: "He will have to make the first move toward me. I will see him but he will have to take the first step." I assured Samuel that I would somehow get his father-in-law to make the first move and ask for Samuel's forgiveness for insulting him. Of course, at the time I had no idea how I was going to do this. But I suspected that Anne's father would welcome reconciliation with Anne's family, at least for his wife's sake.

THE VISIT TO HER PARENTS

In the next session, Anne told me that she had had a telephone conversation with her mother. After the conversation she ate a long piece of string, after cutting it into twenty-five pieces. I told Anne that she must visit her parents, not only for her own sake but for the sake of her children, who would benefit from a relationship with their grandparents. Anne said there were obstacles because her parents lived so far away and a visit would be costly. But after several weeks, Anne herself realized she could not stop her self-destructive behavior until she settled the situation with her parents. She resolved to visit them, despite the cost.

Twelve weeks after beginning therapy, Anne announced her determination to visit her parents. Then she said that at the mere thought of visiting her parents she had tied together pieces of string in a chain a "yard long" and chewed them. I helped Anne rehearse a phone conversation with her mother. I also suggested taking the children with her so they could see their grandparents. Anne said that, although she would like to take them, she thought her husband would not allow it. I encouraged her to go alone if he would not allow the children to go. The next morning Anne phoned me and said she had booked a flight to visit her parents, but she would have to go without the children because her husband objected. She was fearful of going without taking any string with her. I said not to take string with her, but she could reach me by telephone at any hour if she needed comfort from the pain. Wouldn't she agree that conversation with me was healthier than eating string? Anne agreed and did not take string on the trip.

After a few days Anne called me. She said she had talked and wept with her parents until late at night, and her father was willing to apologize to her husband. Her father said that he had not realized that his remark was so offensive and that he had not meant to offend Samuel so deeply. He claimed to have no prejudice against Jewish people. Anne waited a day before trying to phone her husband. Finally, she did and asked him if he would accept his father-in-law's apology. He said he would, and Anne's father sincerely apologized to Samuel, assuring him that he meant no offense.

Some months later, at my urging, Anne took her children to visit her parents. A month after that, Anne asked Samuel if he would accompany her and their children to pay a visit to her parents. They did, and Samuel and her father were cordial to one another. There were no arguments or unpleasant incidents. Anne's parents were able to enjoy their grandchildren, and Anne felt very relieved to have her whole family together in one room. Anne reported that her mother was delighted to be with her grandchildren and seemed to be less depressed than on her previous visits.

After the reconciliation between her husband and father, Anne no longer ate string and therapy was terminated. The course of therapy had taken seven months. Three months after termination I did a telephone follow-up and found that Anne had not eaten or chewed a single piece of string. Relations with her parents were friendly and she was planning to visit them for two weeks with her husband and children over the summer vacation. Anne felt that she was taking more control of her life. She had joined a health club to keep fit, found a better job, and had taken a wonderful vacation in Europe with her husband. At a follow-up session eight months after termination of therapy, Anne had not eaten a single piece of string. She and Samuel had taken their children to visit Anne's parents. Samuel had no problem staying at their home and had been on friendly terms with Anne's father. Anne said that her mother did not seem to be depressed and had enjoyed being with Anne and her children.

THE FUNCTION OF THE SYMPTOM

In my framework for thinking about therapy, a symptom is most usefully viewed as a message about a problem to be solved and as an analogical communication about the nature of the problem, a metaphor (Haley, 1976). It is often useful to think of a symptom as serving a function in a family system. In the case I have described, my hypothesis was that the function of the symptom was to reunite Anne with her parents and her children with their grandparents. Anne's symptom was also protective, in that it benefited her severely depressed mother, who became less depressed when she was able to see her daughter and grandchildren. Saying that Anne "planned" her symptomatic behavior in order to reunite her family and help her mother sounds odd, since the behavior was compulsive and therefore out of her control. But if we look at the end result, it is "as if" Anne had planned the symptom, since it was the only power she felt she had to reconcile her family. Changing the interaction between Anne's husband and her father made Anne's symptom unnecessary because there was no longer an obstacle to interaction with her parents.

From another point of view, one can think of Anne's mother or both her parents as eliciting the symptom from which they eventually benefited. Instead of thinking in terms of a linear sequence of cause and effect, the therapist thinks in terms of reciprocal sequences or mutual interaction in a system. The therapist is then saved from addressing paradoxical questions like who in the family initiates a sequence of interaction, the symptomatic daughter who gets help for the mother or the mother who benefits from the daughter's symptom. The connection is reciprocal. We may think about it this way: if Anne's mother were not depressed and obese, and if it were not so difficult for Anne to visit her, then Anne might not have developed the dangerous symptomatic behavior.

METAPHORICAL SEQUENCES

Sequences may repeat in families, with each sequence expressing another sequence metaphorically (Madanes, 1984), sometimes over many generations. The same reciprocal sequence of a depressed mother who is abusing her body and abdominal symptoms in a daughter is reflected in Anne, her mother, and Anne's own daughter. Madanes (1990) points out several "interactional" functions of metaphors — to communicate, to displace, and to promote closeness and attach people to one another. In this case, the symptom served all of these functions: it communicated Anne's need for connection with her parents; it displaced her pain about the breach with her parents as a focal point for therapy; and, in the end, it served to reunite her family. It is interesting that in the course of therapy with Anne and Samuel another reciprocal sequence came to light. Just as Samuel had held a grudge against his father-in-law, not speaking to him for many years, so had he held a grudge against his own father and had not spoken to him for many years. Unfortunately, Samuel's father had died before his son could become reconciled with him.

THINKING REFLEXIVELY

When we think about reciprocal sequences of behavior in families, our thinking is of a different order than thinking about metaphors in dreams or in symbols (Madanes, 1984). We are not attempting to interpret a metaphor *outside* a system of signification, to map it to an objective reality, past or present. We are not searching for its "true" meaning in another domain. We are reflecting on a construction of signs, and our thinking is located within a domain of signification or analogical communication. Within this domain we construct a reality which, in a sense, may be thought of as "softer" than the reality of hard facts that empirical science has constructed. It is a reality that has a different logic, a different grammar than that of the empirical construction of factual reality. The analogical domain is difficult to describe logically because, like Alice through the looking glass, we keep slipping between levels of classification. Our mode of thinking is reflexive, subjunctive, and hypothetical, and our thinking is connected with our goal or purpose — the problem we are trying to solve in therapy. We ask ourselves for what sequence of behavior might the presenting symptom be a metaphor, so that we may create strategies to solve the problem.

Our analogical model of human behavior is one in which systems play a larger role than individuals. We see behaviors and situations as mutually reciprocal within a system, rather than as causally related discrete events. This is a different approach from the commonsense point of view, which suggests that an individual is the causal agent of his own behavior. As Jay Haley (1990) observed:

> It would appear possible that relationships are formed, perpetuated, and changed according to laws or rules over which the individual in the relationship has little or no control. (p.189)

This view suggests that the notion of causal agency, based on a materialist and atomistic view of human behavior, is no longer a useful model for therapy. A systemic point of view allows us to introduce the notion of reciprocity, replacing that of causality, to find patterns of meaning in events. Repeating sequences, which are reciprocally related in that they metaphorically reflect one another, is one pattern or structure in our analogical model of human behavior. It is an aesthetic pattern, one we would be more likely to seek out in poetic literature than in everyday life.

CHAPTER 7

Repentance and Reparation in a Case of Sexual Abuse

THIS IS THE STORY of a terrible sexual crime committed against a young boy and the reparation of that crime in the process of therapy. The therapeutic procedure is analogous to a kind of ritual process,[6] in particular to what Turner has called a "ritual of redress," which makes right a misdeed in the past. As in all rituals, which employ symbolic acts, the therapy process included symbolic acts of repentance and reparation.

As the therapist in this case, I drew upon the sixteen-step treatment strategy for sexual abuse designed by Madanes (1990), which emphasizes both symbolic and real acts of repentance and reparation on the part of the offender, as well as therapy for the victim of abuse. Madanes' treatment strategy requires the therapist to be extremely directive, following the sixteen steps in the given order.

---

[6]George Stone first pointed out to me the similarities between Madanes' sexual abuse treatment method and Turner's notion of ritual.

In using this strategy, I was somewhat more directive than I usually am in therapy. But I chose to use Madanes' strategy because I thought it was especially appropriate for this particular case. In large part, I chose to use this method because it takes into account the spiritual dimension of sexual abuse and draws upon the healing properties of symbolic acts in the dimension of spirituality.

Madanes' method for treating sexual abuse reflects the view that there is a close connection between sexuality and spirituality and that sexual attacks are also analogical assaults on the spirit of the victim and of the victim's family. This emphasis on spirituality brings the sexual crime into a religious and ethical domain, opening up the possibility for redress in a private setting rather than in the courts. The therapist must of course take care to see that legal requirements, such as reporting a sexual crime against a minor, have been fulfilled. In the case I discuss here, the victim was an adult at the time of therapy, and therefore the involvement of the authorities for a crime against a minor was not an issue.

The treatment method also assumes the inseparability of the individual and the family. Sexual abuse is viewed as a violation not only of the victim but also of the victim's family. Thus, the victim's family must be involved in the treatment, and individual therapy for the victim is only one phase of the therapy.

Madanes emphasizes that the phases of treatment must be followed in the precise order she outlines so as to minimize resistance on the part of the offender. This unchangeable order of the phases of treatment is suggestive of the invariable order of a ritual. In this therapy for the redress of a sexual crime we find also an experiential link between therapy, redressive ritual, and drama. In the therapeutic process, the stages of treatment were very like the script of a play. Therapy was a discrete unit of experience similar to what Turner has called a "social drama." In fact, I had by my side in the therapy room a handwritten "script" with the order of treatment steps. As the social drama of therapy unfolded, I felt it necessary to follow the script carefully, allowing only minimal deviations from it. This drama-like quality gives the process a sense of being removed from mundane daily life and technological routine. And, like a drama, it provides a vantage point for reflexivity, for seeing oneself from a perspective "outside" oneself.

It was clear to me that the power and success of this therapeutic procedure sprang in large measure from its ritual and dramatic quality. The stages of "social drama," according to Turner's schema, are breach, crisis, redress (which includes the subphase of liminality), and reintegration or schism. Using the metaphor of social drama for therapy is especially suitable, for it suggests that therapy, like drama, constructs a separate reality that is "sealed off" (as Turner puts it) from mundane, everyday reality. As in Greek tragedy, the focus of the drama is not so much on events of the past, whether real or mythical, as on the *meaning* or significance of past events in the present — in particular, what symbolic acts of reparation must be performed and what healing must take place within the family. Ritual has the power to transform a family construction of reality into a new state of being. Secret misdeeds, resentments, and pain smoldering beneath the surface are brought out into the open for the first time. Where once there was secrecy, now there is communication. Where once there was shame, now there can be forgiveness and trust.

Comparing therapy in technologically advanced postmodern society with the ritual processes of so-called "primitive" societies may seem a far-flung analogy. For ritual usually involves a belief in mystical beings or powers. These kinds of beliefs are not exactly prevalent in our society. Yet if we consider the epidemic numbers of cases of incest and child sexual abuse in our society, numbers with which every therapist is becoming increasingly familiar, we begin to see our society in a new light. Postmodern society, although advanced technologically, is not immune from the most primitive and savage kinds of crimes. What appeared to Freud and his contemporaries as merely a fantasy or myth of incest appears to the postmodern therapist as the harsh reality of sexual crimes against children in unimaginable numbers. And so it would seem reasonable to look to primitive societies and ancient wisdom to discover ritual methods for the reparation of primitive crimes.

This does not imply that therapy should embrace mysticism or superstition. Therapy needs only to recognize the continuity between the material world and the spiritual world, between sign and object, symbol and symbolized. According to Dewey (1934), originally spirituality was not severed and dissociated from the material world, but was continuous with it. In ritual and and the ritual use of symbols we find this continuity preserved. Dewey writes:

> For many persons an aura of mingled awe and unreality encompasses the "spiritual" and the "ideal" while "matter" has become by contrast a term of depreciation, something to be explained away or apologized for. The forces at work are those that have removed religion as well as fine art from the scope of the common or community life. (p.6)

A sexual offender may believe in a higher power and a higher justice, even though he continues to abuse, repeating compulsively the pattern of his own victimization. His physical actions are severed or dissociated from his spiritual side. Therapy, with its roots in ritual, may reestablish the original connection between the spiritual and the physical. Therapy may invoke an offender's belief in a higher spiritual power and a higher justice and give him the strength and the community support he needs to repent and change his behavior.

The Abuse

When Frank was eleven years old, his father's best friend came to stay at his house for a weekend to look after him and his younger brother and sisters, while his parents attended a conference in another town. His father's friend, whom Frank and his siblings had always called "Uncle Ben," was such an old and dear friend of his parents that he seemed to be a member of their family. The two families were often in each other's company. That weekend, Ben's wife had taken their daughters for a visit with her mother in Canada, so Ben had offered to baby-sit. Late at night when everyone was asleep, Uncle Ben came into Frank's bedroom, climbed into his bed, and performed oral sex on him. Uncle Ben's sexual advances toward Frank continued whenever he and the boy were alone. Their sexual relationship lasted for seven years. This relationship was confusing to Frank, as he had always respected and admired his father's friend, who was a leader in their church and community. A part of Frank knew that what Ben did to him was wrong, and a part of him was frightened by it. But Frank did not know what to do. Since Frank's father was a hospital administrator and his mother was a nurse, he knew that his parents would have to report the abuse if he told them about it. He wanted to spare them the shame and embarrassment of this. He felt the need to protect them as well as his "Uncle" Ben. And so Frank remained silent.

Eventually Frank broke away from the relationship with Ben and began dating a girl at his high school. They had a sexual relationship, for which Frank's strictly religious parents severely criticized him. When Frank was twenty, he met Emily, and after two years of living together they married. While they were dating, Frank told Emily that he had been sexually molested, but did not go into detail. Ben and his family had since moved to another state, and Frank had no contact with him. Frank and Emily had a baby daughter, and the abuse receded into the background of Frank's mind.

When Frank and Emily had a second child, a son, four years after the birth of their daughter, Ben and his family moved back to the Boston suburb where Frank and Emily lived. Ben now played a large part in their social life. He and his family were invited to family celebrations at the home of Frank's parents. Frank grew increasingly uncomfortable being around Ben, but still he said nothing. It was only when Frank saw Ben pick up his little son that he knew he had to do something. Though he was fond of Ben and especially fond of Ben's wife, despite all that had happened, Frank was terrified that his own son would be victimized.

THE VICTIM COMES TO THERAPY

Emily was the first member of the family to seek therapy. She was experiencing suicidal thoughts and other symptoms of acute depression. She felt too depressed in the mornings to go to work and was worried about losing her job at a bank. Emily told me that she had become depressed shortly after the death of her stepfather six months ago. At around this same time, her husband Frank had told her the details of being sexually molested by his father's best friend. She had known before their marriage that her husband had been molested, but only now did she know that Ben had been the molester. This was upsetting her, both for her husband's sake and for the potential danger to her son. The grief at her stepfather's death and the grief at her husband's abuse were both factors in her depression.

Emily came to therapy by herself for several weeks. What emerged was that she was terribly worried about her mother, who had been grief-stricken when her husband died. I could see that Emily's depression was a metaphor for her mother. Emily's talk of suicide was also an attempt to get her mother to pull herself together. I helped Emily think of more positive ways in which she could help her mother. One thing she did was phone her mother's friends and ask them to invite her mother to have lunch or go shopping every day. This cheered her mother up. Emily also encouraged her mother to go back to college to take the classes she needed to update her teaching credential. Eventually her mother did this.

Emily was also very worried about her husband, and to some extent her symptoms were also protective of him. He was talking to her more frequently about the sexual abuse. I told her that I thought this was a great burden for her and asked if her husband might want to come to therapy. Emily looked very relieved when I mentioned this possibility. She said she thought Frank would be willing and even grateful for a chance to talk about the abuse with someone besides her. After Emily spoke with him that evening, Frank called me to make an appointment.

In the first session Frank spoke with relief of the many years of being sexually abused by Ben. He remembered feeling particularly bitter about Ben's demands for anal sex, which he had found very painful and eventually refused. He would at times take out his anger by performing anal sex on Ben. Frank was now thirty-two, and before he confided in me he had never told anyone about the abuse except his wife. He felt that he had dealt with it pretty well by himself; in his opinion, the process of thinking through those terrible years had raised him to a higher spiritual and intellectual level. He also felt that, despite the horrible things that were done to him, he had been able to move beyond anger and the need for revenge to a feeling of compassion.

Frank felt especially ashamed and guilty because the sexual interactions had continued until he was seventeen. I had to remind him many times that he was molested when he was an innocent child and could not hold himself responsible in any way. He had done nothing intentionally to provoke the sexual assaults against him. When I suggested that he confront the offender for the sake of his own healing, Frank protested that Ben and his wife were his parents' best friends. He did not want to upset his family.

I attempted gently to persuade Frank that it was best for him to unburden his soul and speak of the abuse to his family. Sometimes Frank would cancel therapy sessions or simply not show up. I would then phone him, and he would schedule another appointment. I felt that I needed to be persistent for several reasons. First, I was truly concerned that Frank's own son and perhaps other children in the parish were in danger of being abused if Frank remained silent. Frank and I both feared that after Frank had broken away from the relationship Ben might have turned to other children. I was also concerned that Emily would continue to be seriously depressed and suicidal until the matter of the abuse were resolved. She, too, feared that her baby son could be molested if she were not constantly on guard. Most of all, I could sense Frank's relief at finally talking about the abuse to me. I thought he would feel better if his family knew about the abuse and could apologize to their son for not protecting him as parents should have done. But of course the final decision would have to come from Frank.

Following the general principle that all secrets must be violated in cases of sexual molestation of children (Madanes, 1990), I urged Frank to disclose the secret, if not for his own sake then for the sake of his own children and other children who might have been molested or were in danger of being molested. Frank confessed that he had feared for a long time that his younger brother might have been victimized by Ben as well. He wanted to ask him this in the presence of his family.

Finally, one day Frank came into my office and said that he had made the difficult decision to ask his family to come to a therapy session. He had felt so cut off from his family for so many years with the secret of the abuse between them. Now he welcomed the opportunity to share this part of his life with his family in the hope that they would understand him better. He particularly wanted his parents to understand the reason for his sexual behavior during high school, for which they had so strongly condemned him. To make Frank more comfortable with the task of disclosing the abuse to his parents, I went over the proposed steps of treatment with him. He told me that the steps made sense to him and that he felt comfortable with the procedure.

REDRESS

A few days later, I met with Frank's family: his wife, parents, younger brother, and two younger sisters. Since the family did not yet know about the abuse, Frank wanted to tell them about it privately first, without the offender being present.

When his family arrived at my office, I greeted each family member by name and thanked him or her for coming to the session. Then I asked Frank to recount to his family what had occurred. As he spoke, he looked to me often for guidance and support. He seemed to have doubts about whether his parents would believe him. Whenever possible, I asked Frank to use very explicit language to describe what Ben did to him. I asked him to describe the oral and anal sex, the fondling and masturbation, the secret places where he and Ben would meet. At first, Frank had great difficulty talking about sexual acts in front of his conservative parents, as this talk obviously was making them very uncomfortable. It could not have been more removed from topics discussed in their daily life. But I encouraged Frank to continue because it was very important that Frank's parents understand precisely what had been done to him. As he told his story, his sisters began to cry.

When Frank finished his account of the abuse, I asked each family member to say in his or her own words why what Ben had done to him was wrong. Usually the offender would be asked first, but since the offender was not present I began with the victim. Frank said the worst thing about the offense was that his childhood had been stolen from him. Everything went smoothly, with each member of the family finding reasons the offense was wrong until it was the turn of Frank's father, who was clearly in denial of the sexual offense. He began a discourse on why he did not feel angry about what happened, speaking at length about the Christian virtue of forgiveness. He almost sounded as though he blamed his son, the victim, rather than the perpetrator of the offense. In a certain sense Frank's father seemed to be taking the place of the offender in the family, since it is usually the offender who is in denial and has difficulty explaining why the abuse was wrong. Since the offender had been his closest friend for many years, Frank's father had difficulty accepting as true Frank's account of the offense.

After letting Frank's father speak for a few minutes, I had to interrupt him and insist that he try to find some reason why the offense was wrong. I emphasized that there was no doubt that what his son was saying was the truth. Frank's father could barely bring himself to find anything wrong with the offense, saying that we are all sinners and should not pass judgment on others. I could feel myself getting very angry at him, and I could feel the rising anger of everyone in the room except, strangely enough, Frank. Frank looked very peaceful and calm, as though a burden had been lifted from his soul. Frank's father did not say anything more. When it was the turn of Frank's mother, she said angrily that nothing short of murder could be more wrong than what had been done to her son. She was very angry at Ben.

I then agreed with all of the reasons that had been stated and added that the offense was wrong for one more important reason. It was wrong because it caused Frank, the victim, many years of spiritual pain, because spirituality and sexuality are closely connected. The family understood this easily since they were religious and spiritual people.

I decided to skip step four in the usual procedure, which is explaining that a sexual attack also causes a spiritual pain in the victimizer. I felt that given the father's attitude of denial, it was premature to elicit a spirit of empathy and forgiveness for the victimizer.

Step five in the order of treatment steps is the revelation that there is another victim in the family, sometimes one of the victim's parents or a sibling. Neither Frank's father or mother believed they had been molested when Frank asked them. Frank's father, surprisingly, alluded to sexual problems in his marriage, for which he and his wife had sought counseling some years ago. Frank's brother expressed a fear that he might have been molested by Ben; but he did not remember any incidents of abuse. Later, with his own therapist, he came to the conclusion that he had not been molested. Frank's sisters were certain that they had never been sexually abused.

After this discussion, I pointed out that the offense against Frank caused a spiritual pain not only in him, but in every member of his family. A sexual attack on the child the family loved was a spiritual attack on all of them. None of the family had difficulty understanding this and agreeing with it. Since the offender was not present at this session, I postponed step seven, in which the offender must apologize on his knees in front of the victim. I did ask the other family members to get down on their knees and apologize to Frank for not having protected him. Frank's mother readily fell to her knees and apologized to Frank for not protecting him. Frank's father was reluctant but when I insisted he finally did apologize sincerely.

We discussed the possibility of other children in the community being molested by Ben, as all of us were concerned about this possibility. We agreed that the priest of their church should be brought into the process of treatment, and we would ask him to serve as protector of other innocent children at risk. The family wanted to meet with the priest as soon as possible, although they feared that the priest would not believe Frank's story.

I then raised the subject of reparation or restitution for the sexual offense. Although nothing could compensate the victim or the victim's family for what had been done, a symbolic act of reparation was still necessary. This act of reparation should be a considerable sacrifice for the victimizer and a significant help to the victim. After some discussion of what amount of money would be fair to the victimizer yet helpful in a real way to the victim, Frank and his family decided to take some time to think about this and discuss it among themselves.

I said that the next step was for Frank to confront the victimizer in the presence of his family if Frank felt that he was prepared to do this. Frank said he was ready for a confrontation and expressed a preference for confronting Ben alone first, with only me present, before bringing in his family. This was a modification of the usual procedure, but I saw no harm in it and agreed. I wanted to give Frank as much control of the therapy process as possible. At the end of the session, which had lasted two and a half hours, Frank said with a smile on his face: "This has been the best day of my life, because finally I can talk to my family." Frank said that the secret he had held in for so long had put a distance between him and his family that could now be bridged. Frank's mother came over to me and shook my hand with tears in her eyes. She expressed her thanks that this had finally come out and that her son was able to speak openly to her now.

REDRESS, PHASE II: REPENTANCE

Frank phoned Ben and asked him to come to my office, briefly explaining that he wanted to address their former sexual relationship. Ben expressed concern about confidentiality, and Frank assured him that what was said would be confidential. Ben agreed to come to a counseling session on the day and time Frank specified. Given the perpetrator's willingness to come to the session, I suspected that Frank's father had spoken to him first and assured him of his support. In any case, Ben arrived at the session early. He was seventy-one years old, pale, his eyes downcast. He admitted his misdeeds with little prompting from me and answered Frank's questions honestly. Frank asked, "Why me?" "Why at that time?" "Did I do anything to seduce you?" All the questions that had been plaguing him for so many years poured out. The offender assured Frank that everything that occurred was his, the offender's, fault, that Frank had done absolutely nothing to solicit his sexual attention. This situation was quite unusual in that the offender did not imply, but even categorically denied, that he was provoked by the victim. Answering Frank's question about why Ben chose him to molest rather than someone else, Ben explained that he had felt sexually aroused on a number of occasions when he was near Frank.

It was very clear to me as I watched the interaction between the two men that Ben loved and cared for Frank, despite having molested him. Madanes' view that a sex offender often has a kind of disordered thinking, conceiving of the sexual molestation as romantic and somehow not inappropriate, seemed to fit Ben's attitude precisely. Although he took full responsibility for the seduction, Ben kept looking for indications from Frank that he had in some way gotten pleasure from the sexual and emotional involvement. Frank responded to this by saying that although certain aspects of the relationship were pleasurable at the time, even flattering, what Ben had done to him was terribly wrong because he had been an innocent child. And this wrongness was what he wanted to focus on now, not on any pleasure he might have had in the relationship.

The old man agreed with this. He also assured Frank and me that he had not molested Frank's brother or any other children. He admitted to having had homosexual affairs with other men, but not with children. In response to my questioning him about his current sexual outlets, he said that after the relationship with Frank he had turned to his wife for sex. When I asked if the offender himself had been the victim of sexual abuse, he replied that his stepfather had sexually abused him when he was eleven years old. This was precisely Frank's age at the time of the first molestation. Ben said that after the first incident he kept away from his stepfather as much as possible. However, Ben began to engage in homosexual acts with some of his school friends. At the end of the session Ben agreed to meet with Frank's family to apologize, but he preferred not to have his wife present. Frank accepted this.

Present at the next session were Ben, Frank, Frank's wife, his parents, his brother, and his younger sisters. I summarized step two in which each member of Frank's family had stated why the sexual offense was wrong, and I asked the offender to now state why what he had done was wrong. Ben did so without hesitation, saying it was wrong of him to take advantage of an innocent child who had been entrusted to his care. He added that there was no excuse for what he had done. He was relieved that it had finally come out so he could seek help for himself, both emotionally and spiritually. He only hoped that his wife and family would be able to forgive him.

I told Ben that the offense had caused a pain in the heart of the victim and the victim's family, and Ben was able to agree with me that this was so. I continued with step seven and asked the offender to apologize to the victim on his knees, in a powerful symbolic act of repentance. The offender readily fell to his knees and apologized very sincerely, both to the victim and to the victim's family. This was a very powerful and moving moment. The room was so quiet that one could have heard a pin drop. It was clear to all of us present that this sad old man on his knees in front of Frank was sincerely penitent. The victim's father reframed the act of humiliation as a "manly act of apology."

In step eight, I asked the victim's parents to apologize again on their knees to the victim. Here the offender interrupted, objecting that the offense had nothing to do with them, that it was not their fault. He alone was the guilty party. I insisted that Frank's parents could have done more to protect their son. Frank's parents, even his father, apologized to Frank without hesitation. Frank's father had clearly come a long way since the last session. He no longer denied the severity of the offense to his son and almost humbly apologized for not protecting him as a father should have done. He told Frank that he should have been closer to him as he was growing up, and that he hoped there was still time for him to be a better father to Frank.

Modifying step nine, I discussed the legal consequences of molesting children and told the offender that he was indeed fortunate that the victim had not brought this out when he was still a child. The offender agreed that this was fortunate for him. He agreed to go to a therapist for help to insure nothing like this would happen in the future. The offender followed through on this, phoning me later for a referral for therapy. Next, I concentrated on whether the victimizer had molested any other children. He said he had not and voluntarily offered to resign his position as youth leader at the church and soccer coach for the high school so that he would have no further contact with children.

Step ten, in which I see the victim alone in therapy, will be discussed below.

At one point Frank told the offender that he wanted to disclose the offense to the parish priest. The family wanted to ask their priest to act as protector (step eleven) for other children in the church who came into contact with the offender. Frank wanted me to speak to the priest as well. The offender agreed to our speaking to the priest. In my first conversation with the priest, his first impulse was to deny that such a thing had happened. But when I told him that the offender had confessed and repented, he accepted that it was true. He then became concerned that Frank might want to publicly humiliate the offender, which would bring disgrace to the church. I felt confident in assuring him that Frank did not intend to do this. He did not have vengeful feelings against Ben. I told the priest that I thought Frank had moved beyond anger to a higher level of spirituality. The priest finally agreed to meet with Frank and his family and to act as protector for other children in the church. This was carried out, with the victim, the victimizer, and the victim's family all talking with the priest, who agreed to monitor the victimizer in the hope of preventing further molestation.

The next step, reparation, was briefly discussed during the session with Frank's family, and it was agreed that the victim and the victimizer would meet in my presence to agree on the kind of reparation that would be made. I emphasized that the reparation was a symbolic act, for nothing the offender could do now could possibly compensate the victim or the victim's family for what he had done. Nonetheless, there must be reparation both as a powerful symbol of the offender's repentance and to help the victim in his life in some way. The reparation should constitute a long-term sacrifice for the offender and a long-term benefit for the victim.

REDRESS, PHASE III: REPARATION

The reparation process was the longest stage in the therapy, mainly because Frank wanted not only Ben but also Ben's wife to feel the necessity for substantial financial reparation. Frank initially had trusted that her religious and ethical sense would motivate Ben's wife to offer reparation voluntarily. He turned out to be wrong about this, as she was very resistant. She could hardly believe Frank's story, and so I asked her husband to assure her that it was the truth. She bitterly opposed financial reparation, insisting that Frank was merely being vengeful. In one session, I asked Ben's wife to imagine how she would feel if her own sons or daughters had been sexually molested while they were children. I asked Frank to describe in explicit language the sexual acts, the fear, and the pain he had felt during the years of abuse. But Ben's wife still could not believe the truth of what Frank was telling her.

Gradually Frank's attitude changed from being loving and protective toward the offender's wife to impatience and anger. Like Frank's father, the offender's wife was all too ready to step into the role of victimizer. She insisted that reparation was unfair, because their financial situation was worse than Frank's at the present time. All of their financial resources were being drained by her mother's illness. She accused Frank of "blackmailing" her husband with the threat of making the offense public. Her husband, on the other hand, said he was very willing to pay the reparation Frank asked for and trusted that Frank would not publicly denounce him.

In individual therapy, I helped Frank to separate in his own mind the issue of reparation from the issue of public denunciation of the offender. Frank's feeling was that he did not feel the need to make the offense public so long as the offender was in therapy and there was no chance of there being other victims. He felt no need to cause the offender any more humiliation or pain than he had suffered already. Reparation was a separate matter for Frank. He felt that the molestation was responsible in some way for his lack of success, as he had had learning problems at school dating from the time of the molestation. In particular, he had developed a learning disorder in arithmetic. Learning disabilities are fairly common among children who have been sexually molested. Madanes (1995) argues that this is because the child has to utilize so much mental energy to keep the abuse secret that he cannot concentrate well at school. Financial reparation would help Frank overcome some of the failures that his disability had caused. It would allow him to go into partnership with a friend of his who owned a small printing business, something he had always wanted to do.

After many agonizing sessions, some of which included Frank's parents, a reparation of $40,000 was agreed upon. In addition, the offender also agreed to pay for Frank's counseling sessions. The amount of reparation was set by Frank in consultation with his family. Frank had been saving for several years to start his printing business. This sum was what he still needed. It was important that the amount constitute a real sacrifice on the part of the offender and a real benefit to the victim, something that would help him in a significant way, such as starting a business. Everyone was aware that Frank could take the case to an attorney to be tried in civil court, but Frank insisted that this would only be a final resort if a reparation agreement could not be reached privately. Frank's faith in the process of healing and his need to forgive made him reluctant to take the matter to a judicial setting.

REDRESS: PHASE IV

Step thirteen involves the therapy of the offender, and this I preferred to refer to another therapist, even though the offender asked me to see him and his wife in therapy. I did suggest to the offender a strategy that Madanes (1990) has called the strategy of good deeds — that is, the offender should give something to the community such as volunteer work at a convalescent hospital. This strategy may help the offender forgive himself, the last step of the procedure. The offender was so penitent, ashamed, and depressed, it was remarkably easy for me to feel empathy for him, despite the horrible crime he had committed. I became very concerned that he might not forgive himself and resort to suicide. I shared this concern with the priest. The priest, who had also been concerned about the possibility of the offender's suiciding, agreed to give him his support. With the priest's encouragement, the offender entered therapy. He continued to meet with the priest and attended a religious retreat for healing his spirit.

SCHISM

The remaining steps of treatment, according to Madanes' model, are restoration of love for the offender, restoring the position of the offender in the family and helping the offender forgive himself. In the present case, these are still open-ended. The offender went to a religious retreat to help with spiritual healing, and to therapy for emotional healing and repairing his marriage. Eventually he and his wife told their grown children about the offense. This had to be done so that their children could be protected. Since the offender was not an actual member of the victim's family, but only a very close friend, the step of reintegration into the family may never take place. At the end of the final reparation session with the offender and the victim, the offender said he hoped Frank would someday be able to forgive him. Frank told him that this would take a long time, but that he too hoped he would be able to forgive. The process concluded with schism rather than reintegration into Frank's circle of loved ones, since Frank and his wife decided they did not want to have any further contact with the offender for a long time. They both wanted to get on with their lives and leave this behind them. Frank's parents did not want to have any more contact with Ben.

OTHER ISSUES: LIMINALITY

After the process of reparation, Frank continued in therapy for two months, mainly in individual sessions but at times with his wife. The therapy had opened up other areas that Frank wanted to change in his life. In this respect, the redressive phase of therapy constitutes a kind of liminal stage, "betwixt and between" the structural past and the structural future. It is also an occasion for reflexivity, for viewing one's past life and values from a vantage point "outside" one's usual point of view. The past organization of his marriage, in which Frank had played the role of his wife's victim, was no longer acceptable to him. Frank confessed to me that Emily had verbally abused him ever since they got married. "I am a victim by nature," he said sadly. It was as though Emily had fallen into the role of victimizer which Frank's story seemed to require.

To help him change the situation and his image of himself as a victim, I suggested that Frank construct a plan to leave the scene whenever Emily verbally abused him. His "safe place" for retreat was to be his aunt's house. He was also to tell her that he would not put up with any further verbal abuse. This strategy worked, and Emily stopped abusing him. Another issue for Frank was Emily's constant threats to leave the marriage if he didn't do what she demanded. He and I came up with a strategy to deal with this problem. The next time Emily threatened to leave, Frank would agree with her that she should leave if she felt she had to. Up to now he had been placating her and begging her to stay. Whenever she threatened to move back to her mother's house, Frank said "OK." This tactic soon put an end to her threats. As it turned out, Emily had herself been a victim of verbal and physical abuse by her father. When this fact came out in therapy, Frank became more understanding of her past behavior in their marriage. What also emerged in therapy was that Emily's father had abandoned her mother when Emily was twelve years old. Her mother had raised her and her two sisters alone, and they had suffered many hardships until her mother remarried.

The process of therapy helped Frank achieve a new level of self-respect and strength in his relationships. He emerged from the liminal phase of therapy with a new image of himself. He was no longer willing to accept an abusive or victimizing relationship in any form. He felt that in many ways he had been victimized by his parents, especially when they had condemned him for having sexual relationships before marriage. Entering therapy as "a victim by nature," Frank emerged from it transformed into a confident person, unwilling to put up with being victimized in any way.

Frank ended therapy when he felt that his goals had been achieved. He planned to devote his energies to his wife and children and to his new printing business. I encouraged him to focus on the good things in his life, such as his children, his successes in business, his future plans to travel with his wife, and so forth. I pointed out that the years of abuse constituted only a small fraction of the course of Frank's life; he had many happy years to look forward to. The process of therapy, from the initial session with Frank's wife to termination with Frank, was five months, with one-hour to three-hour sessions at irregular intervals.

CONCLUSION

Madanes (1990) notes that if the therapist goes through the sixteen steps of treatment in the correct order, there is little resistance on the part of the offender or the victim's family. This fact was strikingly true in this case. Even I was surprised at the offender's lack of resistance and his willingness to repent. Similarly, Frank's father moved from a position of denial of the sexual abuse to acceptance of Frank's story in a very short time. As I said earlier, I attribute these changes to the ritual power of the therapy procedure. The atypical behavior of the offender may also have been influenced by a number of other factors in this particular case. For example, the offender feared public disclosure of the offense, which would have destroyed his career and his standing in the community. Also, I think that because of his own spiritual development and stage of life, the offender was spiritually and emotionally ready to repent and to ask for forgiveness at the time of the confrontation. At some level, not entirely sealed off from the rest of his personality, the offender knew that what he had done was wrong. Because he believed in God, he wanted to atone for what he considered to be sinful behavior before he died and met his Maker. In this sense, the ritual invoked and utilized the offender's belief in a higher power removed from the secular world.

Although the process of therapy was certainly an ordeal, the offender felt a sense of relief that it had occurred. When therapy ended, he was able to begin a journey of self-forgiveness. The offender had very clearly welcomed my guidance as to what was right for him to do in order to help the victim and absolve and heal himself. The offender instinctively seemed to trust that the victim, the victim's family, and I would treat him fairly and mercifully rather than vengefully, if he truly repented. And he was right. Clearly everyone in Frank's family felt a great deal of love for the offender, which did not suddenly vanish when his offense became known. He had been a beloved member of their family even though he was not related to them by blood. The decision to have no further contact with him, at least for the time being, was a painful one.

The treatment method, which includes empathy and even support for the perpetrator while requiring his repentance and humiliation, was especially suitable for this case. To my surprise, I was able to feel real empathy for the perpetrator of this horrible crime against a child because he was sincerely penitent. And the perpetrator was aware of the empathy I felt for him and trusted me because of it. I do not think the process would have gone so smoothly if I had not been able to feel empathy and even pity for the offender.

Resistance on the part of the offender's wife might have been avoided if I had involved her earlier in the therapy process. Or perhaps, as I have come to believe, it was this very role reversal, in which the offender's wife took on the anger, resistance, and denial usually typical of a perpetrator of sexual abuse, that freed the actual perpetrator from the role of victimizer and allowed him to repent and seek absolution.

The treatment method was successful for another important reason. The steps and focus of the therapy process seemed to resonate with the subjective experience of the victim. Frank was a religious person. For him, the sexual offense signified a spiritual violation as much as a sexual violation. A therapy that did not include spirituality and symbolic acts of repentance and reparation would not have been meaningful and healing to Frank. Frank needed to feel in control of the therapy as much as possible, checking at each stage that the steps were spiritually and ethically correct for him. He wanted to be very clear in his own mind that he was acting mercifully and not vengefully, in accord with his view of himself as a Christian and a merciful person. Frank truly had been raised to a higher spiritual level through the long years of silent suffering. The coinciding of the steps of treatment with Frank's own experience of his personal healing process gave him a sense of being in control, reversing the situation in which for many years he had been out of control.

The link of the therapeutic procedure I have just described with what Turner (1986) called "social drama" should be apparent. It may be useful to quote more at length here Turner's description of "social drama":

> A person or subgroup breaks a rule, deliberately or by inward compulsion. . . . Conflicts between individuals, sections, and factions follow the original breach, revealing hidden clashes of character, interest, and ambition. These mount towards a crisis of the group's unity and continuity unless rapidly sealed off by redressive public action, con-

senually undertaken by the group's leaders, elders or guardians. Redressive action is often ritualized and may be undertaken in the name of law or religion. Judicial processes stress reason and evidence; religious processes emphasize ethical problems. . . . If a social drama runs its full course, the outcome . . . may be either the restoration of peace and "normalcy" among the participants or social recognition of irremediable breach or schism. (p.39)

Like a drama, the therapy of repentance and reparation constructs a reality outside of or, as Turner puts it, "sealed off" from the mundane routines of everyday life. The crossover point between the liminal space of therapy and everyday life outside the therapy room is the victim's *experience*. The experience essentially involves reflexivity—seeing one's past and present life from a new point of view outside of or transcending one's everyday life. The person's experience of himself is essentially transformed. In Frank's case, therapy had the effect of helping him get over the guilt and shame he had felt for years about the sexual abuse that had been perpetrated against him. As a result, he was able to feel closer to his family, resolve problems in his marriage, and move toward forgiving the perpetrator of the crime against him, which as a Christian he very much wanted to do.

CHAPTER 8

The Hub of the Wheel: Therapy as a Rite of Passage

I'm the hub that makes the whole wheel work.

— Young man in therapy

THE ATTEMPT OF A young person to disengage from his family and leave home to start his own life often precipitates a family crisis. The young person becomes symptomatic or behaves in destructive ways, and the parents feel helpless and out of control (Haley, 1980). When this kind of situation occurs, therapy may be necessary to bridge the stages in the life cycle, from the stage of a child living with his parents to that of an adult living on his own. Haley has compared therapy at this stage to an initiation ceremony. Therapy thus may resemble what van Gennep called a rite of passage.

Perhaps therapy has come to perform the function of a ritual because our society offers few public symbolic occasions to help young people make the difficult transition from childhood to adulthood. In the introduction to van Gennep's now classic work, *The Rites of Passage*, we read:

It seems . . . likely that one dimension of mental illness
may arise because an increasing number of individuals are
forced to accomplish their transitions alone and with private symbols. (1960, p.xvii)

Van Gennep believed that the transition between childhood and
adulthood did not necessarily occur at physical puberty but could
occur at other ages as well. He distinguished between *physical puberty* and *social puberty* (1960, p.68). In our society we find young
people well beyond the age of sexual maturity, sometimes in their
thirties and forties, living at home because they are unable to disengage from their parents and pass into the responsibilities of
adult life. The young person wavers over-long in a kind of liminal zone betwixt and between the social worlds of childhood and
adulthood. A young person may engage in behaviors that appear
bizarre or mad, such as violence, suicide attempts, intoxica-
tion with alcohol or drugs, hearing voices and seeing visions that
people around him don't perceive, and so forth. In such a case,
therapy may be a useful and necessary step to help the young person make the transition from social childhood to social adulthood.

In the following, I give an account of a therapy that performed
the function of a rite of passage in van Gennep's sense. As in ritual
contexts, the therapy involved metaphors, symbols, and analogical
thinking. Symptoms are viewed as signs or analogical communications about the youth's social context — in particular, the interactions between his parents in a troubled marriage. In this view, a
symptom is understood as protective and stabilizing in a family
system, focusing attention away from volatile issues that are not
being addressed in the larger system, such as problems in the parents' marriage.

HIERARCHY

The young person's symptom, especially if it is severe, produces
an inversion of the family hierarchy. Instead of the parents' having
control over their offspring (as is appropriate in the case of a child

living at home), the young person controls his parents, with the whole family becoming organized around the symptom and the parents feeling helpless and out of control. In this type of case, the notion of hierarchy is a useful construction because it gives the therapist a tangible focus in the therapy. Hierarchy is not an absolute and unchanging aspect of families. It is, however, a construction applicable to many families in our culture who come to therapy. The goal for the therapist is to restore a hierarchical arrangement in which the parents regain control and help their offspring disengage and leave home. In many respects the parents must treat the youth as a child again to accomplish this goal. Only when the parents are in control can the young person move out and enter a stage of social adulthood in which he and his parents become social peers. In addition to correcting the hierarchy such that the parents are in charge, the therapist helps the parents communicate directly with one another instead of analogically through their offspring (Haley, 1976).

CELEBRATIONS OF MEANING

Important stages in the life cycle are marked, in most societies, by celebrations. Life transitions such as birth, puberty, marriage, and death all have ritual celebrations associated with them to signify a new state of being or incorporation into a new group. Certain symbols and symbolic acts or behaviors are associated with the transitional person. Turner, in his study of Ndembu rites of passage or transition, points out that the person in transition is defined by a name and a set of symbols (1967,p.95). In our society, ceremonies and parties celebrating high-school graduation may serve to mark the passage from social puberty to social adulthood. In cases in which the transition of leaving home is especially difficult and requires the help of a therapist, it is often useful to mark the act of leaving home with a party or a celebration of the young person's "graduation." I often recommend that the young person and his family plan a celebration together in a therapy session, with the party taking place when the youth moves out of his parent's home into a new situation.

THE "HUB OF THE WHEEL"

Andrew was a twenty-five-year-old young man living at home. He was the youngest of four sons. His brothers had left home, found jobs, married, and were doing reasonably well. Andrew, however, was having difficulty making a transition to the adult social world. When he was seventeen and in high school, he began to use alcohol and marijuana, and a year later he had an automobile accident while drunk. After Andrew recovered from his injuries, his parents kicked him out of the house because he would not work or go to school. Andrew lived with a friend and worked part-time as a store clerk until he had another automobile accident, again while drunk. He lost his job and returned home to recuperate. He was able to graduate high school through a continuation course at home.

This cycle repeated itself a number of times over the course of seven years. Andrew would move out, become ill or injured, return home, and when he was well enough to get around would engage in alcohol and marijuana use until his parents kicked him out. Andrew had been jailed twice and had not had a driver's license for several years. At various times Andrew's parents had tried counseling for him, but nothing seemed to help.

At the time the family consulted me, Andrew had been in therapy intermittently for more than four years. He was coming home drunk almost every night, sleeping until noon, and doing only minimal chores around the house. At his parents' request he had enrolled for two courses at a nearby community college, but he attended classes only sporadically. Andrew's parents felt helpless and out of control. They were afraid that if they kicked Andrew out of the house again he would have another automobile accident resulting in injury or death.

THE FIRST SESSION

Andrew accompanied his parents to the first session as I had requested. My goal was to form a hypothesis about why Andrew was behaving in such a way that he could not leave home. What social context problem was Andrew performing or acting out with his destructive behavior? If I understood the problem between the parents, then I could address in therapy both Andrew's symptoms and his parents' problems simultaneously. My best source of information about the parents' problem would be Andrew himself, for he, I assumed, was bringing them to therapy. In my experience, young people always know what the larger problem is, and they will communicate it to me if they feel that they can trust me to help their parents.

When the family arrived at the session, I asked Andrew's parents for their permission to spend a few minutes alone with their son to better understand the nature of his problems. In asking their permission to speak with their son, I was implicitly putting the parents in a higher position in the hierarchy, symbolically giving them authority over him.

Andrew was a tall, blond young man, dressed in torn jeans and a tee-shirt. He was unshaven, and his hair reached his shoulders. But despite his unkempt appearance and his many failures in life, Andrew seemed like a very intelligent young man to me. I assumed that on some level he was quite aware that his behavior was helping his parents by distracting them from more serious problems. In our private conversation, I asked Andrew if he was worried about his parents. He said he was not, and just wished they would leave him alone. I then commented that sometimes young people help their parents by giving them something to worry about. In spite of Andrew's tough, angry, and frankly frightening demeanor, I saw a glimmer of recognition in his eye when I said this. He understood that I could see that he was helping his parents, but he was not going to admit this to me directly. I decided to engage him in a discussion of literature, since his father had told me that Andrew seemed to take a particular interest in a Shakespeare class he was taking. "What is your favorite Shakespeare play?" I asked him. Andrew, interpreting my question as more than a question of mere fact, replied with a very reflexive metaphor, *"The Tempest."* Andrew was using language poetically, collapsing the name of the play and the reality of his parents' tempestuous marriage. Now we knew where we stood, Andrew and I.

I next asked Andrew what sorts of things his parents were likely to have fights about, since everyone knew that all couples have fights in the normal course of married life. Andrew replied that his parents' arguments were mainly about him. His parents rarely saw one another, so they had little to fight about apart from him. I could then hypothesize that Andrew sensed that if it were not for him and his problems, his parents would not talk about anything at all. Andrew's father stayed at the office longer than he had to on weekdays and worked on Saturdays; he traveled frequently for his job. Andrew's mother kept busy with a part-time job and an active social life with women friends. Their busy schedules allowed them little time together. "I'm the hub that makes the whole wheel work," said Andrew, metaphorically expressing how the family system was organized around him and his problems. "You don't need to be the hub of the wheel anymore," I responded, using his metaphor. "Your parents have hired me and it is now my job to take care of them and help them solve their problems. Your job is to get on your feet and make a life for yourself. You have a lot going for you." Andrew shrugged and said nothing, implying that I didn't know what I was in for. How right he was.

DEFINING THE GOALS OF THERAPY

After the first session, I met with Andrew's parents alone, only occasionally having Andrew join the sessions. The first thing I asked them to do was to get a clear statement of the problem they wanted to solve in therapy. The problem was to be stated in nontechnical terms, so that the parents, and not only myself as an expert in a technical field, would feel capable of solving it. After a short discussion, Andrew's parents said that their primary goal was to get their son to stop drinking. Other goals were for Andrew to get a job and satisfy the mandates of the court so that he could get his driver's license back. I suggested that moving out of the house might be an additional goal, but Andrew's mother objected to this, saying that Andrew was stable now, whereas if he moved out he might injure himself again. Andrew's mother seemed to perceive the threat to the stability of the system posed by her son's leaving home. Andrew's father disagreed with his wife and thought Andrew should move out as soon as possible. He was tired of supporting his "lazy, good-for-nothing son."

Emphasizing that the parents must be a united front in order to solve Andrew's very serious problems, I suggested we leave the issue of moving away from home until the other goals on which they had agreed had been achieved. The important thing in my mind was for the parents to agree on *something* so they could work together cooperatively to help their son. Andrew's drinking was a good focus since they both agreed that it was an important goal.

GETTING THE PARENTS IN CHARGE

I asked Andrew's parents if they were willing to make a sacrifice to help Andrew stop drinking. They said they would do anything. I then asked if they would be willing to have a dry house, with no alcohol of any kind on the premises. If they wanted a drink, they would have to go to a restaurant. They agreed to this. I then told them they must sit next to their son while he called each of his friends on the phone. The parents were to instruct Andrew to tell each of his friends that he wanted to stop drinking and wanted his friends to help him by not taking him out to bars or other places where he could drink. The parents agreed to this as well. I told Andrew's mother that she should oversee that Andrew attended the driving classes required by the court. She objected, saying that this would require her to drive him to the classes and wait for two hours until he finished to drive him home, since there was no other transportation available. I told her she would have to make this sacrifice because she loved her son and wanted him to succeed in life. Finally, she agreed.

I also told Andrew's mother that she would have to drive Andrew to his classes at the community college, wait for him, and drive him home. Reluctantly she agreed to do this as well. We then agreed on a consequence if Andrew were to come home drunk again. If he did, he would be confined to the house for a week, except for the classes his mother drove him to. I predicted that he would test this, so they should be prepared to enforce it. They would have to back up one another and form a united front to enforce the rule about drinking. I suggested that mother and father spend one hour together three times a week, preferably away from the house, discussing how they would keep Andrew under control.

This directive had the dual purpose of helping their son and forcing the parents to communicate with one another.

Over the next few months, my meetings with Andrew's parents focused on getting control of Andrew and getting him to his court-appointed classes. His mother conscientiously drove him to class, waited in the parking lot outside the classroom, and then drove him home. On several occasions Andrew came home drunk. His parents then confined him to the house but did not enforce it. When I gave suggestions as to how they could enforce this rule, one or the other of them would sabotage my suggestions. Usually they would agree in the end to the tactic I suggested and then simply not follow through on it at home.

Hoping to motivate Andrew's parents to follow my suggestions, I began to focus on what a financial drain Andrew was on the household. This had the effect of motivating father. He began to attack his wife for not being a good mother. Finally, mother said she would take time off work to stay home and enforce Andrew's house confinement, but only if her husband would not work on weekends so that he could take charge of Andrew and give her a break. He agreed, and stayed home from work several times to monitor Andrew. This put an end to the episodes of coming home drunk.

Finally, Andrew's mother became so fed up with driving Andrew around and staying home with him that she too agreed that her son should look for a job and think about moving out. I suggested that Andrew's father oversee that every morning Andrew spend at least two hours looking for a job. I suggested that Andrew should collect job applications during the week, and on Saturdays his father would direct him in filling them out. This served the additional purpose of having father stay home on Saturdays instead of going to the office, which was something his wife bitterly complained about.

Father followed through on helping Andrew, who got the first job he applied for, as a clerk in an electronics store. He had to take the bus to and from work, since he was not yet entitled to get his driver's license back. The job turned out to be very satisfying to Andrew and he seemed to be doing well. He met other young people who worked at the store, including a girl he seemed to like.

Andrew's self-esteem improved as he performed his job well. His appearance changed to reflect this. He was neat and well-groomed, his hair cut short, and he wore new clothes.

THE COUPLE

I continued to see Andrew's parents in therapy, for now they wanted help with problems in their marriage. I knew that the underlying anger and resentments between them had to be addressed directly if Andrew were to cease to be their vehicle for communication. There were many deep resentments between this couple, as well as serious sexual problems. Twenty years ago Andrew's father had had an affair with his wife's best friend, for which his wife had never forgiven him. She had had no sexual interest in her husband since that time. The sex they had was infrequent and unsatisfying to them both.

I suggested a ritual of repentance and renewal for the couple, in which father would give his wife a gift such as a vacation, jewelry, or whatever she wanted. This was to be father's penance for the affair he had had. Father thought this was a good idea, and they discussed various vacation possibilities in the session. But he never followed through on any of his wife's suggestions. Instead, he began to talk about his many resentments against his wife, such as his feeling that she wanted to control him and have him do what she wanted him to do whenever he was home. He said this was why he stayed at work so much. His wife agreed to ask less of him when he was home.

As husband and wife began to communicate directly about these issues in therapy, Andrew took more control of his life. He registered for a computer programming class at the local community college. He finished his court-mandated driving classes and on weekends began the community service work required for getting back his driver's license. I knew that Andrew would not get his license until he felt that his parents no longer needed him to live at home. Having a driver's license meant that he would be able to live independently and get to and from work, without being dependent on his parents for transportation. A driver's license was a symbol for Andrew of the independence and responsibility of adulthood. Andrew seemed to be doing well and was not drinking, except for an occasional beer after work with his new friends. I was unprepared for the crisis that erupted.

RELAPSE

Late one Saturday night I received a phone call from Andrew's father. Andrew had had a car accident while drunk. Fortunately he was not hurt, but his parents were very upset. I was puzzled at this news, since things had been going so well for Andrew. When I met with Andrew's parents the next day, they told me that Andrew's paternal grandfather had given him a new car for his birthday. Grandfather gave Andrew the gift without father's permission and very much against his wishes. In doing this, grandfather was upsetting the hierarchy we had been working so hard in therapy to construct. He had undermined the parents' authority, taking away from them the control over their son that they needed in order to help him.

I had to assume that Andrew's failures were helping not only his parents but his grandparents as well, as is often the case. Haley (1980) tells us that a relapse in such a case is predictable:

> When the problem young person begins to obey the parents and the parents are sufficiently united to take charge, there is a reaction from other people involved in the situation. . . . At times the grandparents or other members of the extended family, who have been stabilized by the previous structure, begin to intrude. (p.104)

In this case, Andrew's grandmother had recently been diagnosed with a life-threatening disease. Andrew's problems could be seen as providing a focus to distract family members from this additional problem in the wider family system.

Fortunately, Andrew did not lose his job after this crisis, and he continued to work. Following my suggestion, Andrew's father insisted on returning the car to grandfather and told him not to interfere with Andrew while the family was in therapy. This was the first time he had ever stood up to his father, who was a very powerful and domineering man.

In therapy, I helped mother and father come to an agreement

that since Andrew was working, he must pay something toward his room and board at home. They refused to enforce this for many months. In the meantime, mother began to complain in sessions about how much all this therapy was costing them. I commented that Andrew's paying rent could help offset the cost of therapy. This persuaded mother to drive Andrew to the bank the following day to cash his paycheck and ask for the rent money on the spot. She did, and Andrew paid her the current rent plus some of the back rent he owed. From then on, mother drove Andrew to the bank each month and he paid her rent from his paycheck.

LEAVING HOME

A year after therapy had begun, Andrew still had his job and had been promoted to assistant manager of the store. At one family session he told me that his job was the most satisfying thing in his life. But now a new concern presented itself to me. Mother and father's marital difficulties had not been resolved and father was talking about separating. I attempted to persuade father to stay with his wife to provide Andrew with the stability he needed to keep his job, at least until he felt able to move out and begin a life of his own. Otherwise, I warned, Andrew would still be living at home during his father's retirement and old age. I painted a dark and gloomy picture of father's old age, with his son still living at home.[7] Father did not like this prospect and realized that it was probably an accurate prediction, so he agreed to stay and work on the marriage.

Therapy continued for six more months, a kind of weekly ritual that was frustrating to me since only very minor changes were occurring in the marriage. The couple skillfully managed to avoid all of the direct and indirect strategies that I proposed, making me feel as ineffectual at helping them as they must have felt with their son previously. Yet they seemed glued to seeing me. Soon it became clear to me that I had taken Andrew's place as "the hub of the wheel," providing a source of stability for the couple.

But while his parents were in therapy, Andrew was able to disen-

---

[7] This was suggested by Jay Haley in a personal communication.

gage from them. He began dating a young woman at work and eventually felt a need for privacy in his social life. He obtained his driver's license after fulfilling all of the court-ordered conditions and put a down-payment on a car. Finally, he rented an apartment of his own and planned to move out of his parents' house. Before he did, I suggested that Andrew and his parents plan a party to celebrate his "new life." The party took place at Andrew's new apartment. His parents provided the ingredients for the meal, and Andrew and his girlfriend prepared a lavish banquet for friends and family. Only soft drinks were served as a sign that everyone present supported Andrew's continuing sobriety. Andrew's parents presented him with a gift of a television set for his new home.

Although Andrew's problem had been resolved in therapy, his parent's marital problems had not. Andrew's parents eventually discontinued therapy, and a year later father separated from his wife and moved into his own apartment. Eventually, the couple divorced. Andrew continued living on his own, working and going to college at night. He did not move back to his parents' house.

CONCLUSION: THERAPY AS A RITE OF PASSAGE

Growing up and leaving home is a normal stage in the family life cycle. In the case of a young person having difficulty with the transitional stage of leaving home, therapy may be necessary to help the youth make the transition. In this sense therapy, as illustrated by this case example, serves the function of a rite of passage. This does not mean that therapy is or should be a necessary and natural part of the process of leaving home in our society. Therapy should be invoked only if a young person fails at making the transition to social adulthood in the ways a society usually provides.

In conclusion, I will briefly summarize the type of therapy which may serve as a "life crisis ritual" (Turner) or "rite of passage" (van Gennep). First, the therapist empowers the parents to get control of their offspring. The therapist acts as an adviser, sharing her experience and expertise with the parents. Second, the therapist focuses on the future and solutions to the problem rather than the origins of the problem in the past. She helps the parents formulate the goals of therapy. Third, the therapist focuses on two levels of family organization: the youth's problem and the problem in the youth's social context, which is metaphorically expressed by his problem. The former is a sign or symbol of the latter. Fourth, the therapist helps the youth's parents communicate directly with one another rather than analogically through their offspring. Finally, the therapist helps the family plan a party to celebrate the new social role of their offspring when the transition of leaving home takes place. This celebration incorporates symbols of the problem's resolution and of the young person's new social role.

CHAPTER 9

Children's School Problems

IN THIS CHAPTER I shall discuss four case examples of children having problems at school and how these problems were resolved in family therapy. In each case, as we shall see, the school problem signifies a problem or problems in the child's social context. The school problem is most usefully viewed as serving a protective function in the child's family, focusing the parents' attention on the child's problem instead of on a more serious and painful family problem (Haley, 1976; Madanes, 1981). The child's problem or symptom also helps the parents in another way. It connects the parents with the school, thereby bringing them into contact with professionals who may be able to help them. Thus, the therapist sees the child not as an individual with a problem but as part of a larger system. The child's symptom is not, as common sense would seem to suggest, a symptom of the individual child. It is a symptom of the family, the larger organic whole of which the child is a part.

The main objective in cases involving school problems is for the therapist to empower the parents and put them in charge of solving their child's problem (Haley, 1976). The therapist's role is best seen as that of a consultant to the parents, to help them come to agreement about the steps they will take together to take charge of their child. An important goal of therapy is for the parents to learn to cooperate with one another rather than disagreeing on matters involving the child. Often a cycle is set up in which parents disagree on how to correct a child's problem. This parental disagreement in turn produces an escalation of the problem, which produces more disagreement and blame between the parents. The therapist's goal is to break this cycle by helping the parents or other family members come to agreement.

LANGUAGE IN THERAPY

Language plays a significant role in this approach to children's problems. First, the kind of language that the therapist uses is critical in achieving the goal of getting the parents in charge of the problem. Words like "depression," "attention deficit disorder," "phobia," or "gender identity disorder" put a child's problem into a clinical domain, where only a therapist has expertise. Words like "sadness," "lack of attention," "misbehavior," "lack of confidence," or "developmental issue" bring the child's behavior into the domain of everyday life, where parents may feel more capable (Madanes, 1981).

But second, and even more critical, the therapist must use language in such a way that *it does not crystallize a behavior or set of behaviors into a permanent problem with a label.* A behavior can be changed. A problem persists over time and gathers momentum. It may even come to be viewed as an attribute fixed irrevocably by the child's genetic code. As we have seen in Chapter 2, words and other signs have the power to create realities that are illusory. The fundamental illusion is that the realities created by signs are permanent and unchanging. Over time (and with adequate cooperation from the media), these illusions of permanence may become false and distorting idols, such as the idols of the marketplace that Francis Bacon described. That is, labels affixed to the self are signs that create a picture in people's minds of something that does not in fact have objective existence. These labels or diagnoses, these objectified illusions, become marketable commodities or designer diagnoses. The static and objectifying labels that are applied to children's problems are such idols, because they do not adequately portray the fluid reality of the child. Children are extremely flexible and adaptable, able to grow and change even more than adults. We have only to look at children's games and notice the delight children take in changing and varying the rules each time they play. The extent to which children's "disorders" are created and maintained by using the static language of entities to describe their behavior is unfortunately underestimated. When diagnostic signs or labels are not applied sparingly and provisionally, they begin to take on a life of their own. They take on the appearances of entities or objects. Narrative therapists White and Epston (1990) have identified something like this kind of phenomenon with what they call "the objectifying of persons." They argue very cogently that such objectifying should be avoided in therapy. Therapists should conceive of problems as "external" to the person, rather than as internal attributes of the personality.

CONTEXT

Instead of labeling children, I believe that it is more useful to look carefully at the contexts in which the problem behavior occurs and also at the contexts in which the problem behavior does not occur. Sometimes a child will perform poorly in a class because she has a personality conflict with a particular teacher. Or, as Madanes has pointed out, sometimes a child may begin to misbehave when her father returns home in the evening in order to deflect father's attention from problems he has been having at work. Or she may be deflecting father's attention, thereby preventing him from arguing with his wife.

It is also the case that what may in fact be normal childhood behaviors become intolerable to parents under the stress of marital or other kinds of problems. A child's uncontrollable behavior may become magnified in the parents' minds, as they begin to feel less and less in charge of the child. Finally, the parents may consult a professional to help them get control of their child, rather than focus on a marital relationship that is out of control. The child's behavior then may become crystallized as an objective "diagnosis" and fixed irrevocably with a label, with the result that the child's behavior becomes even more difficult to change.

The probability that this kind of pattern will be enacted is increased by the fact that parents naturally want to feel that they are not to blame for their children's problems. Many parents are noticeably relieved when their child receives a concrete diagnosis such as "attention deficit disorder." The parents may then believe that their child suffers from an illness that is beyond their control, the cure for which is medication and not a change in parental behavior. In my own experience, parents will go to unbelievable lengths to avoid the feelings of guilt and shame that come with believing they are in some way responsible for their child's problem.[8] After many unsuccessful experiences in trying to talk parents out of their child's diagnosis, I have found what seems to be a more useful approach. Instead of insisting that a diagnosis is incorrect, I generally let the diagnosis stand and offer an alternative point of view on the treatment of the diagnosed "illness." Of course, if it becomes clear that parents don't agree with the diagnosis given to their child, then I will agree with the parents, as in the following case example.

---

[8]Dorothy Bloch (1978) comments on the extraordinary lengths to which parents will go to avoid feeling responsible for their child's emotional problems. She writes: "The most poignant expression I have encountered of the pain suffered by the parents of schizophrenic children was the unspoken hope communicated by one mother that I would declare her son schizophrenic, a condition she assumed had neither cause nor cure. When I indicated after several diagnostic sessions that I thought his condition might be arrested and reversed by psychoanalytic treatment involving a repatterning of her way of handling him, she left and did not return for several years. She clearly preferred to think her child was doomed rather than acknowledge having played any part in his illness." (p.128) My own experience of parents of children with severe symptoms is the same as Bloch's. A serious diagnosis is often preferable to my suggestion that family therapy would solve the child's problem, because family therapy implies that the parents are somehow involved with the child's condition.

CRYING AT SCHOOL

Ten-year-old Susan was referred to therapy by her teacher because she cried at school almost every day. The teacher had tried many things to help Susan, hugging her, reassuring her, and encouraging her to talk about what was bothering her, but nothing worked. Susan's teacher thought that Susan might be upset about her older sister, who, according to Susan, had hit her on a number of occasions and once had threatened to kill her. When Susan wrote stories, they were usually about her sister. When I asked the teacher when Susan had first started to cry at school, the teacher replied that she "had always done it." Susan's other teachers said that she had cried in their classrooms for the past two years. The teachers told me that they thought Susan was in some way carrying the burden of her family's problems.

When Susan's mother phoned for an appointment, I asked that she and her husband come in to see me alone to give me some family background and a history of Susan's problem. Susan's family consisted of her father, mother, her fifteen-year-old sister Marguerite, and herself. Her father, Enrique, was a repairman for the telephone company, where he had worked for fifteen years. Her mother, Josie, worked at the high school as a librarian. Josie talked most in the session, clearly feeling more at ease in a counseling situation than her husband. Enrique was a physically large man of Central American origin, who had been born in this country and spoke English without an accent. He remained silent during most of the session unless I specifically addressed him. He did say that he had felt helpless about resolving Susan's problem and was relieved to have my help.

Susan's mother thought that the crying at school had begun when Marguerite had started hitting Susan at home, over two years ago. Her parents had taken Marguerite for therapy after a violent episode when she had threatened to kill her sister and had chased her into her room. The therapist had given Marguerite a diagnosis of "paranoid schizophrenia" and referred her for psychiatric treatment. However, mother and father did not follow through with this recommendation because they thought the diagnosis was too strong. Mother learned to control Marguerite's violent outbursts by never leaving the sisters alone together in the house. She also put a lock on Susan's door so that she would feel safe in her room.

If Marguerite's violent behavior toward Susan were connected with Susan's crying at school, I knew that I would have to get an understanding of why the violence began in the first place. What family problem was being masked by Marguerite's outbursts of violence? Was the violence a metaphor for the parents' relationship or was there some other volatile relationship in the family that Marguerite's behavior signified? So I asked Susan's parents what else had occurred at around the time that the violence began. They told me two important facts. First, three years ago they had moved from Boston to a suburban area, buying a house on the same street as Enrique's sister and her family. They were delighted that their daughters would be able to live near their cousins, with whom they were good friends. Secondly, Enrique's sister had become violently angry at Enrique and Josie because they had not attended Christmas dinner at her house. Josie, Enrique, and their daughters went instead to Josie's parents for the holiday. Apparently, Enrique's father had been offended by this as well, and he had barely spoken to Enrique or his family since that time.

Enrique admitted that he was particularly hurt by his father's ignoring Marguerite and Susan since the incident. His father would come to visit his sister's children down the street but would not stop in at Enrique's house. I asked Enrique if there was anything that could be done to reconcile his family with his father and sister. Enrique replied that he did not think that would be possible, as his father was a proud and stubborn man and he, Enrique, was unwilling to make the first move because he felt so hurt. Enrique's mother had died ten years ago, and since that time, according to Enrique, his father had never been the same.

For the moment, I decided to leave aside the major issue of family reconciliation and focus on getting Enrique and Josie in charge of Marguerite's behavior. My goal was to reorganize the hierarchical arrangement in the family such that the parents would cooperate in taking charge of their daughter. By defining Marguerite's violence as a behavior problem, I was making it something the parents had the power to control. A behavior problem can be solved more easily than "psychosis." I asked the parents to do the following. First, they would clearly state to Marguerite the rules she must follow with respect to Susan. She was not to yell at Susan, hit her, or in any way threaten her. If she did, she would have to do a half-hour chore to help the family. I got out a pen and paper, and together we made a list of chores that could be assigned to Marguerite. In addition to a chore for hurting her sister, Marguerite would have to buy her sister a small gift by way of apology. Josie agreed that she would accompany Marguerite to the store to oversee her picking out a gift. I discussed these consequences with Josie and Enrique, asking them if they were willing to enforce them together. They said that they were.

To help Susan get over her sadness, I directed Josie to see to it that her daughter laughed every day. She was to take Susan to the public library and check out books of cartoons and humor. Then she and Susan would read a book together every evening. She was also to read the comics in the newspaper with Susan. Josie cheerfully agreed to do this. By describing Susan's crying as a sign of "sadness," I was bringing it out of a clinical domain and turning it into an everyday kind of thing that her parents could handle. Finally, I asked Josie and Enrique to bring their daughters with them to the next session.

The family session with the girls present was a kind of microcosm of the life of this family. Whenever Josie or Enrique began to speak, Marguerite would interrupt in some way, either by speaking or by glaring at her sister and gesturing to her. Whenever she did this, I asked Enrique to tell her to stop her rude behavior. When the subject of the girls' aunt, Enrique's sister, came up, Marguerite and Susan had a lot to say. They felt that their aunt and their grandfather were being hateful to their parents. Most of the session was dominated by the topics of hurt and protection in this family. For example, when I suggested that Enrique might like to see his father more often, Marguerite objected that her father could not trust her grandfather, for Enrique had been hurt before by his father's "suddenly turning cold and distant" after they had been close for a time. Susan agreed that Enrique was better off without a relationship with his father, because the old man had been so hurtful to his son. I began to form a hypothesis that Marguerite's violent behavior was a desperate attempt to focus her parents' attention away from the hurt caused by the breach with their aunt and grandfather.

Over the next few weeks, Marguerite's behavior improved with her parents' enforcement of her having to do chores for misbehavior. Mother also supervised her in purchasing several small gifts for her sister. Marguerite complained bitterly about this, but she did it. Susan cried at school less and less until she stopped crying altogether. She also told me in a session that lately Marguerite seemed to be more "normal." She and her sister began to get along better, and Marguerite even invited Susan to go to a movie with her, which delighted Susan. But the thorn in the flesh of this family, the alienation from Enrique's father, kept coming to the surface. When Enrique's father had heard about his granddaughters' problems, he had written to Marguerite, sending her a gift of money for her sixteenth birthday. Enrique was hurt by this, because his father had always ignored Susan's birthday, favoring Marguerite. But for Enrique the larger issue was that his father seemed to favor the children of his sister over his own children. At the next session, Marguerite brought me a copy of a letter she had written to her grandfather.

> I received your birthday card today. And thanks for the card but personally I had mixed emotions when I read it. It made me feel a lot of hurt and pain that I've been trying to push away for some time. I don't think I've ever really thought of you as a grandfather, but more as the father of my father that doesn't want to have anything to do with his son's family. It seems to me and my sister that you always give our cousins gifts and take them places on their birthdays. But if we're lucky, maybe we'll get a card. And you also ignore my father. You don't even remember him on his birthday. You've not only hurt me and my sister, but you have hurt my father too. And that's not fair. I have one question to ask you. What did we ever do to you to make you not want to even try to get to know us?

With this, it became clear to me that, however difficult the task would be, I had to bring about a reconciliation between Enrique's family and his father. At my next meeting with Josie and Enrique,

I asked them if they would be willing to invite Enrique's fath
therapy session. Enrique was reluctant at first, but I assured ...ı
that it had to be done for the sake of his daughters. I believed the
girls would continue to have problems if the rift between their
father and their grandfather were not resolved. After I said this,
tears came to Enrique's eyes. "Why does this have to hurt my kids?
My relationship with my father has nothing to do with them," he
said hopelessly. The sight of this large man in tears moved me very
much. This family's hurt seemed to have no boundaries — what
Enrique was feeling seemed to pass right into Marguerite and Susan. Finally, for the sake of his children, Enrique reluctantly
agreed to have his father come to my office. I asked that only the
parents be present at the session with Enrique's father.

Enrique's father arrived early for the session. He was a tall,
dark, and very dignified looking man. When Josie arrived without
Enrique, I was concerned that he had changed his mind and decided not to come to the session. But a few minutes later Enrique
came in, looking very nervous. I explained to Enrique's father that
for the sake of his grandchildren it was important that the differences between himself and his son and daughter-in-law be resolved.
Enrique tried to explain to his father that the favoritism he showed
to his sister's children was hurtful to his daughters, and that he
wished his father would treat all the cousins equally. At this, his
father became very angry. He began to shout at Josie that she had
kept him from seeing his grandchildren at Christmas two years ago.
He accused her of doing too much talking and not letting Enrique
speak up. When Josie began to defend herself, grandfather became
so angry that he abruptly got to his feet and left the room. Enrique
then burst into tears, saying it was useless to try to speak about
feelings with his father. Josie said that she had been afraid something like this would happen and hoped I was not offended.

But we all had underestimated the magnitude of the love in
this hurting family, for just then an astonishing thing occurred.
Enrique's father came back into the room. He sat down and apologized to me for leaving, saying that he had needed to go outside
and cool off. Then he said, "When I die, I will not be able to leave
buildings or monuments with my name on them. All I have to leave
behind are my grandchildren. I will do what I can to help them to

lead happy normal lives." With some part of his being, grandfather understood that his behavior was affecting his granddaughters. During the rest of the session, grandfather listened to my sugges- tions as to what had to be done for the sake of Marguerite and Susan. I suggested that he avoid favoritism among the cousins and spend roughly equal time at the homes of Enrique and his sister. I also suggested that grandfather ask his daughter to become friend- lier with Enrique's family and that he put away his resentments toward his daughter-in-law.

After this session, things began to change for this family. Grandfather sent Susan a belated birthday gift with a friendly note. Enrique and his father began to speak on the phone once a week. Enrique went to visit his father. After a few months, Josie invited her father-in-law to Sunday dinner at their house and he came, bringing gifts for Susan and Marguerite. The girls' aunt became friendlier toward them, inviting them into her home for the first time in more than two years. They were now allowed to play with their cousins. Marguerite no longer hit or verbally abused her sister and began getting better grades at school. Susan did not cry at school again.

I stayed in touch this family for a period of three years, seeing them occasionally during times of difficult transitions. One crisis erupted when Enrique injured his arm and could not work at his regular job for three months. At this time I received a letter from Josie saying that Marguerite was "depressed":

> I am very concerned about her. She is so unhappy. Things are going well for her but that doesn't even make her happy. She made honor roll, and her English teacher nom- inated her for some type of English award. She has a good relationship with her aunt and uncle, and goes over to visit them often. We are planning to invite Enrique's father for dinner before Father's Day, because we are not ready for the whole family to be together. This morning I told Mar- guerite that I hated to see her hurting like this, and have her feel so helpless and out of control of her life. I told her that I was going to call you to see what we can do to help . . . that seemed OK with her.

Knowing this family as I did, I could guess that Marguerite was feeling the pain of one of her parents. When Marguerite did come in to see me shortly after I had received her mother's letter, she complained about "feeling paralyzed." I asked her where in her body she felt paralyzed, and she replied that it was her right arm. Here she was expressing in metaphor how worried she was about her father's injury (also in the right arm) and about how the family would survive with him out of work for so long. I reassured her that everything would be all right, that limbs improved with rest and exercise, and that her father's disability insurance would pay their expenses for the time he was unable to work.

In the next few sessions with Enrique and Josie, I helped them clarify the hierarchical boundaries between them and their daughters. I asked them to reassure Marguerite that Enrique's arm was healing well. Every day Enrique would tell his daughter that his arm felt better and explain how physical therapy was helping him regain strength. Josie was not to express her worries and fears in front of her daughters but was to be hopeful and positive with them. Most important, the parents were not to discuss their financial worries or other difficulties in front of the girls. A few weeks later, they told me that Marguerite was feeling more energetic and was no longer sad. She phoned to tell me that her arm no longer felt paralyzed.

I continued to see Enrique and Josie for almost a year to work with them on marital issues. Marguerite had occasional spells of sadness, but they became less severe and less frequent. She did not hit her sister again. Her grades continued to be excellent, and she won several awards at school. After graduating high school, she enrolled in a community college, where she did very well.

To summarize this case, Susan's crying at school signified a violent situation in her nuclear family, in which her sister hit and verbally abused her, as well as a volatile cross-generational conflict in her extended family. Susan was also terribly worried that her sister might be "crazy." Susan's problem was resolved in two steps. First, I reorganized the generational boundaries in the nuclear family such that the parents were in charge of Marguerite. By asking the parents to spend more time together, I helped them to communicate directly with one another rather than through their daughter.

Second, I worked to bring about a reconciliation in the extended
family, so that grandfather and father were no longer in conflict.

THE BOY WHO SET HIMSELF ON FIRE

Eleven-year-old Alan and his family were referred to therapy by
Alan's school counselor. Alan had been getting into trouble at
school and had been sent out of the classroom to the principal's
office many times. Twice he had been caught smoking cigarettes on
the school grounds and had been sent home from school. The
counselor warned Alan's parents that the next step would be sus-
pension from school. Alan was very bright, but his grades were
below average and he was on the verge of failing two subjects. This
was because of many missing homework assignments in his classes.

Alan's parents had been divorced for several years, and Alan
lived with his mother on weekdays and his father on weekends. His
parents had made this arrangement because the town where mother
lived had excellent schools, much better than those in the nearby
town where father lived. Alan's mother had remarried after the
divorce and had a good job in an insurance company. Alan's father
lived alone. He had a girlfriend, the latest in a series of relationships that never seemed to last. Father had his own business, an
office supply store.

In the first session, Alan's parents told me that they now had an
amicable divorce. Some years earlier they had been very angry at
one another, but they had tried to resolve their differences for
Alan's sake. On one occasion, around the time of the divorce,
Alan had set on fire a cape that he was wearing for Halloween.
Fortunately, his father saw him in the back yard and went running
out to help him. Alan suffered minor burns, and his parents were
very frightened. Since that time, Alan had threatened suicide several times. Alan's parents had taken him to a therapist, who had
diagnosed him with "oppositional-defiant disorder." But a year of
individual therapy had changed nothing. Alan's misbehavior and
poor grades continued. His parents did not know why he was having these problems. To my questions, Alan replied that he did not
know why either. In a session alone with me, he was uncooperative

and hostile. He did say that he thought that his father's business wasn't doing well.

My first suggestion was that Alan's parents keep in close contact with his teachers, to be sure he handed in his homework on time. If he missed an assignment, the teacher should call mother, and she would see to it that he handed it in the next day even if she had to accompany him to the classroom. I then asked that Alan and father attend a session alone with me. My hypothesis was that Alan's failure at school signified some sort of failure in his father's life and that Alan was diverting father's attention from his own problem. Whereas Alan's mother seemed to have reorganized her life after the divorce, Alan's father had had not yet built a new life for himself.

In the session with Alan and his father, many significant facts emerged. One was that Alan's father was about to lose his business because of a series of unfortunate financial decisions. Also, father had begun to drink more frequently, stopping at the bar every day on his way home from work. Alan was clearly very worried about his father, both because of his business difficulties and because of the drinking. He was also worried about his father's health, as he was overweight and had high blood pressure. "You should be taking better care of yourself," Alan burst out, almost in tears. The hostile, reticent young man whom I had seen in previous sessions was transformed before my eyes into a vulnerable child who was desperately worried about his father.

I asked Alan if he had any suggestions about how his father could improve his life. Alan had many good suggestions. He said that his father should go to a health club instead of the bar after work and that he should take steps to save his business. Also, his father needed more fun in his life. He should go out more with friends, instead of staying home and watching television or drinking at the bar. Alan also said that he wanted to live with his father. When his father protested that the schools were better in his mother's town, Alan replied: "What do good schools matter if I am failing anyway?" Father finally agreed to talk to Alan's mother about Alan's moving in with him at the beginning of the next school year. The condition for this would be that Alan brought up his grades at school.

Since I could see that Alan was protecting his father by his misbehavior, I decided to use the strategy of a paradoxical contract with them.[9] My thinking was that if Alan's misbehavior and failure at school were harmful rather than helpful to his father, he would cease this behavior. I could see than there was a great deal of love between father and son and that Alan would not want to do anything that would cause his father real harm. He was also a very intelligent boy, quite capable of doing well at school. I asked Alan and his father to agree to the following contract. For every day that Alan had a day at school with no problems and turned in all of his homework assignments, on the following day his father would go to a health club and work out for an hour instead of going to the bar. If Alan was sent to the principal's office or missed an assignment, father could go to the bar.

Both Alan and his father seemed pleased at this proposal and agreed to it. I wrote up the agreement in the form of a contract, and Alan and his father signed it. Next I had a session alone with Alan's mother and explained the contract to her. At first she was surprised and protested that this situation would place too much burden on Alan, making him responsible for his father's drinking. I told her that I had seen this kind of contract work many, many times, and I asked her to trust me because I knew she would do anything to help her son. "Isn't Alan capable of doing better at school?" I asked her. Mother had to agree that he was capable. Finally, I was able to persuade her to agree to the arrangement for six weeks. If at the end of six weeks Alan were not doing better at school, I promised her that I would try something else.

At the next session two weeks later, Alan and his father told me that only once had Alan misbehaved at school, so his father had gone to the bar only once. The rest of the days father had worked out at the health club he had joined. He announced that he felt much better physically. This strategy continued to be effective, and soon Alan began to get better grades at school. In therapy, we discussed ways in which father could improve his business. Over the next months, Alan continued to do well at school. We had a

---

[9]This strategy is described by Cloé Madanes (1984).

session with Alan's mother and began to discuss the possibility of Alan's living with his father when he entered seventh grade the following year. At first mother protested, but finally she agreed to this if Alan continued to get good grades and had no further problems at school.

Alan did move in with his father, visiting with his mother on weekends. He was much happier with this arrangement. He had no more problems at school and began to make friends. Father managed to keep his business. Eventually he began dating a stable and supportive woman whom he later married.

THE BOY WHO WOULDN'T GO TO SCHOOL

This case is quite unusual, in that I had no direct contact with the identified patient, a boy who would not go to school. I conducted the therapy entirely by means of written directives addressed to the child's parents. One advantage of this rather unusual way of working was that the parents were put entirely in charge of solving their son's problem. This method of therapy by written means is useful for clients who live at great distances from the therapist, as in this case.

One evening, my husband asked me if I could help an old college friend of his who was very worried about his young son. His friend, whose name was Ron, lived in Australia, but business trips brought him occasionally to Boston where we lived. On his last trip Ron had brought his wife, and my husband and I had spent the evening with them. All my husband could tell me was that his friend's ten-year-old son was having problems and had been in treatment for six months with very little improvement. I agreed to meet informally with Ron the next time he was in town to see if I could help.

A few weeks later, Ron called to make an appointment to come to my office. At the session, he told me about the problem his son was having. His son, Brian, was depressed and teary-eyed when he woke up in the morning and had refused to go to school for the past six months. When his mother tried to take him to school he sobbed and lay on the ground. Brian had been seeing a psychiatrist but still refused to go to school most of the time. Occasionally his mother could persuade him to get up and walk with her to school. But very soon the school would telephone and ask her to pick Brian up because he was so miserable.

Thinking Brian's problem would not be difficult to resolve, I offered to help, but only if Ron promised to follow my directions very carefully. I would write down a few simple directions and seal them in an envelope that he and his wife could open together when he got back to Australia. At first Ron became upset. "It's something that I am doing. I knew it all along," he said, obviously in pain. I responded that looking at it that way was not really productive. He was clearly a good father who loved his son very much. I was just going to suggest some simple changes in behavior on the part of him and his wife that in my experience helped children with problems such as his son's. There was no question of guilt or blame. This was a problem that we were all working on solving together.

Finally, Ron reluctantly agreed to discuss my recommendations with his wife, since they were at their wit's end and would do anything to solve their son's problem. He then brought up the subject of my fee. I replied that if my directions did in fact help him and his wife to resolve Brian's problem, they could purchase ten copies of this book and donate them to libraries in Australia. He thought this was a reasonable fee and agreed to it.

That evening I wrote down the following directives: (1) Ron and his wife were to spend one half-hour each evening after the children were in bed making a list of Brian's positive qualities. Every day each parent would tell Brian at least five positive things about himself. (2) Every morning when she walked with Brian to his school, Brian's mother was to tell her son in conversation why she was looking forward to the day. This had to be truthful, so she had to plan something enjoyable for herself every day, such as having lunch with a friend or going swimming. Furthermore, when mother picked Brian up from school she would tell him at least one thing that she had enjoyed during the day. (3) Father was to spend one half-hour every evening alone with Brian, either reading to him or helping him with his homework. I knew that father would have to come home early to do this, as he usually returned from work after Brian's bedtime. (4) During their evening time together, father would tell Brian in conversation at least one thing that father had enjoyed in the course of his day. (5) Neither parent was to yell at Brian or criticize him. They were to be patient and tender with him. (6) If mother and father had any disagreements, they were to discuss them away from the house, preferably in a restaurant. In fact, they should schedule a dinner out once a week to discuss Brian's improvement. Also, mother and father were to take walks together in the evening to discuss Brian's positive qualities. They were to continue to do all of these things until Brian's problem completely disappeared. Finally, I asked that the parents contact me in six months to let me know how Brian was getting along. I put these directives in an envelope, and my husband gave them to Ron, who was leaving for Australia the next day.

My thinking in this case was that Brian was overinvolved with mother and wanted to stay home from school to keep her company. He was worried about mother's loneliness, with father spending so many hours at work. The directives were aimed toward releasing Brian from worrying about his parents, involving father more with Brian so that the boy could disengage with mother, and getting the parents more involved with one another by spending time together alone.

I heard nothing from Ron or his wife Mary for several months, and I wondered if they had done what I had suggested. Then, almost exactly six months later, I received the following letter from Mary.

> At last I am writing to you. I'm sorry I haven't been in touch earlier to let you know how Brian is progressing. Up until about two months ago I was still feeling a little on edge that his problem would return. However, touch wood, he seems to have resumed his old confident self.
>
> We followed your very valuable advice, which thoroughly intrigued Brian. He couldn't understand why we were being so nice to him. After a few weeks we started to see a marked difference and eventually the problem disappeared altogether. Now Brian is confident, loud, naughty, cheeky and disobedient and thoroughly objectionable — a return to the Brian we know and love! He is

happy at school and is getting good grades. So a big thank
you to you Marilyn.

I continued to stay in touch with Ron and Mary by letter for
several months about Brian's progress. His problem did not recur,
and he continued to do well at school.

THE BOYS WHO WANTED TO BE GIRLS

One morning the director of a local nursery school called me.
She said she was very worried about two four-year-old boys at her
school. John and Jeff were twin brothers who had attended her
school for a little over a year. Ever since the director had known
them she had noticed their attraction to girls' toys and girls'
dress-up clothes. She had not been concerned about this at first, as
she encouraged non-sexist behavior in the children. But now the
brothers did nothing else at school but dress up in girls' clothes and
play with dolls. The director noticed that the boys rushed over to
the girls' clothes first thing in the morning with a kind of obsessive
quality. Moreover, they seemed to have no interest at all in playing
outdoor games with the other boys. Finally, the director became
concerned. When she mentioned this to the boys' mother, mother
confessed that her sons did this at home as well, dressing up in her
nightgowns, blouses, and underwear. They never went outdoors,
and ignored the new bicycles that they had received for their
birthday.

The school director was concerned about the boys because the
other children were beginning to notice their behavior. She told the
parents that they might want to consult a therapist about their
sons. The parents wanted her to phone me first, before they called
for an appointment. I told the school director that I would be
happy to see this family.

When the parents called, I asked them to bring John and Jeff to
the first session. The parents, George and Becky, were a delightful
couple, intelligent, attractive, humorous, and clearly wanting the
best for their sons. The boys were slightly built, small for their age,
and fair-haired like their mother. They were dressed exactly alike,
in pink tee-shirts and red shorts. While the boys played with toys in

a corner of my office, George and Becky told me about their family. They were trying to raise their sons in a "non-sexist way," but they were afraid they had gone overboard and were now beginning to be concerned about the cross-dressing. They both noticed that the behavior had a kind of "obsessive" quality about it. George explained to me that he and his wife had been brought up by very restrictive and conservative parents, and they did not want to bring their sons up in this way. But now they were worried that they had inadvertently steered the boys toward homosexuality. The parents had become especially worried when one day John announced that he wanted to "cut his dingus off." They were also concerned because John claimed he had a younger sister named Jenny who had died before he was born but still visited him in his room at night as he was falling asleep.

George and Becky had a traditional kind of family organization, in which George worked and was the breadwinner of the family, while Becky was a full-time mother and homemaker. Her only work outside the home was volunteering at the boys' school two days a week. This was George's second marriage; he had a sixteen-year-old son by his first marriage who visited them every other weekend. George and Becky told me that they wanted their sons to be comfortable with sex and nudity, so that they would not have the same sexual "hang-ups" as they did. They often went around naked at home and did not hide this from John and Jeff. Also, the twins were in the habit of waking up at night and coming into their parents' bed.

As they spoke, I could see that George was more articulate than Becky. He was also more concerned about the cross-dressing. He was afraid that if it continued the boys might begin to identify themselves as homosexual. His feeling was that this kind of choice would lead to unhappiness later in life. Neither parent believed that homosexuality was fixed in a child's identity at an early age. They felt that it was a choice that could be encouraged or discouraged in a child.

When I asked Becky about her interests, she said that she just stayed home and cared for her family. She enjoyed volunteering at the school because it gave her a chance to socialize with the other mothers. She had never gone to college but thought that she might take classes at night when the boys were older. She had few close friends. Apart from church and school volunteering, she had few social contacts. Her husband and her sons were, she said, "her whole life." At the end of the session, I asked the parents to come back without the boys in the next session so that we could discuss ways to change their behavior.

I decided that there were two things to be done in this case. First, a hierarchical boundary had to be established between the parents and the children. I could see that mother was intensely involved with her sons, while father was more peripheral. Father was involved with the boys mainly for discipline. A goal of therapy would be to disengage mother from her overinvolvement with her sons, so that they would be able to engage with their peers. Another goal was to get father involved with his sons in more affectionate ways instead of just for discipline. Finally, these parents needed to be educated about child development, and in particular the development of gender identity. I suspected that in some way mother was covertly encouraging the boys to dress and behave as girls because she did not want them to grow away from her. Because the children were twins, there was a further therapeutic goal of establishing a boundary between the two boys. Twins not only have the developmental task of separating from their mother, but must also separate from one another. Parents can facilitate this separation process in many ways, by dressing twins differently rather than in matching outfits, by giving them different experiences as much as possible, by referring to them as individuals rather than as "the twins," and by noticing and encouraging the unique qualities and strengths of each child.

At our next meeting, I told George and Becky that they had done an excellent job of being enlightened and non-sexist parents. But they had gone overboard in their desire to raise their sons in a non-sexist way. Now it was time to backpedal a little, so that the boys would be more balanced. In my opinion, they needed to develop the male sides of their personalities now that they had nurtured their feminine sides. The parents agreed with this. I asked George and Becky to do the following. First, Becky was to tell her sons firmly not to wear girls' clothes. She was not to smile or laugh when they dressed in her nightgowns, but was to tell them firmly to change into boys' clothes. Also, she was to go to a toy store and purchase masculine dress-up costumes, such as pirate hats and swords, cowboy outfits, and ninja-warrior swords. Becky was to encourage her sons to dress up in these costumes instead of in her nightgowns, and she should give them a lot of approving attention when they did. She agreed to do this. Second, George was to spend twenty minutes every evening with his sons, engaging them in "masculine" activities such as playing ball, building models, carpentry, etc. He was to be very gentle and patient with the boys. In addition, every weekend he should do one "masculine" thing with each of the twins individually. This could be as simple as a trip to the hardware store or playing catch in the park. Also, father should be the one to take the boys shopping for clothes, pointing out to them appropriate colors and styles for boys. He would also encourage them to pick out their clothes individually, rather than buying them matching outfits. The general purpose of these interventions was to construct a reality for the boys in which the cross-dressing could not exist.

Third, there was to be no more nudity in front of the children. The parents should maintain their privacy. They could be nude together alone in their bedroom, but not in the other rooms of the house. Fourth, the boys must learn to sleep in their own beds. If they came into their parents' bed at night, mother was to put them firmly back in their own room. Because bed-wetting had been a problem, we decided that if either of the boys wet his bed at night, mother would supervise him in washing and drying his bed sheets and pajamas and remaking the bed. Fifth, I suggested that the boys needed their own space at school, so Becky should take a break from volunteering in their classroom. This would give her time to do something she always wanted to do, like take college classes. Here I was trying to make sure that mother was not unintentionally encouraging the girlish behavior at school.

Finally, I suggested that George and Becky get a baby-sitter and go out together one evening a week without the children. This, I hoped, would get them to communicate directly with one another.

After a few weeks, the parents reported significant improvement. The boys were delighted with their new dress-up costumes. They had expressed an interest in taking karate lessons, which they had heard about in school, and Becky enrolled them in classes. The bed-wetting had stopped. John no longer talked about the sister who visited him at night. At school, they had begun to play with boys' toys and no longer wanted to dress up in girls' clothing. But although at school John and Jeff were becoming more interested in trucks and trains, there were still times when they wanted to wear Becky's nightgowns and blouses at home. I hypothesized that in some way mother was covertly encouraging them to do this.

A few days before my next appointment with the family, Becky phoned to say that George would not be able to come to the appointment because he was going on an overnight camping trip with his older son. I suggested that Becky come in without him. In our conversation, Becky expressed some resentment about her stepson. He was an excellent athlete, and a straight A student. George always took time off to go with him on class trips and occasionally took him camping. "George must be very proud of him," I remarked. Becky responded fiercely, "He's very proud of John and Jeff too." My chance remark seemed to have affected her strongly and was, as it turned out, a decisive turning point in the therapy. She replied that she wanted her husband to be as proud of her own sons as he was of her stepson. I replied that her husband had many years to be proud of John and Jeff. They were bright boys and would no doubt do well at school. Father was already proud that they were behaving more like boys at school.

After that session, Becky began to firmly scold the boys when they took out her clothes. Eventually they stopped trying to dress up in her clothes at home. A few weeks later, the school director reported that John and Jeff no longer took any interest in girls' toys or girls' clothes at school. They had started to play outdoors with the other boys, which was very unusual for them. I continued to see mother and father in therapy and suggested that George take some "boy-type" outings with John and Jeff, such as camping or fishing trips. After several weeks, there had been no further incidents of cross-dressing at home or at school.

Mother and father then said they would like to continue to see me for marital therapy. In one of the sessions, Becky expressed her anger and resentment that George seemed to favor his older son over the twins. George had been unaware of this, but after thinking it over he admitted to feeling very guilty about his divorce and trying to compensate his older son. He agreed to try to change his behavior. George's main complaint in therapy had been that Becky had been sexually distant from him since the birth of John and Jeff. I suggested that perhaps she would be more responsive sexually when he took more interest in their sons. After three months, George and Becky reported that they were getting along much better, and we decided that therapy could be terminated. We agreed that I would make follow-ups by telephone to be sure that there were no recurrences of the boys' cross-dressing or playing with girls' toys.

At a three-month follow-up, father told me that John and Jeff no longer showed any interest in girls' toys or clothes, either at home or at school. They seemed to love choosing their own clothes and shoes at the store and always chose "boy" colors. The boys had gone on two weekend camping trips with him, which they all had enjoyed very much. Mother told me that the boys were continuing with karate lessons and would be starting Little League teeball in the spring. She added, "George is very proud of them." Mother had registered for two classes at the local community college and was enjoying them. She felt that she was beginning to have a life of her own apart from her family. Eventually she got a part-time job as a receptionist in a doctor's office, which she enjoyed very much. After a few months she was promoted to office manager.

Nine months later I received a card with a photograph of John and Jeff in baseball uniforms with big grins on their faces. The card said:

> We are playing teeball this year. John is on the A's and I am on the Orioles. We like tee ball a lot. We also take karate. We miss you.

I continued to be in touch with this family for two years, and there were no further episodes of cross-dressing or interest in girls' toys. I happened to meet the school director at the grocery store one day, and she told me that the boys were consistently participating in sports and boys' games.

LETTERS IN THERAPY

Reading over this chapter, I became aware of how often I receive letters from my clients, so perhaps it makes sense to say a few words about the role of letters in therapy. I do not deliberately use letters as an integral part of the therapy process. In this respect, letters play a different role in the type of therapy I do than in, say, the narrative school of therapy, which consciously employs narrative means (White & Epston, 1990). Clients generally write me letters or cards for three reasons: to summarize and clarify the results of therapy; to keep me up-to-date on their progress and let me know if there has been a relapse that should be addressed; and, occasionally, simply to stay in touch.

In a more general sense, written language as such is less privileged, that is, less creative, than spoken language in my view. Similarly, language used poetically or metaphorically is more creative than language used in a denotative way.

Epilogue

IN HUMAN LIFE THERE IS the paradox that we are both determined and free. Our early experiences in our families, our culture, our gender, and our race seem to determine our experiences later in life and the ways we relate to other people. Just as in the Greek tragedy Oedipus could not escape the fate the oracle declared for him at the time of his birth — that he would kill his father and marry his mother — neither can we escape our own fates, our own stories. Our early experiences with our parents, and even our parents' early experiences, along with our genetic heritage, determine much of the course of our lives. But Sophocles' Oedipus, having suffered his cruel fate, devotes the rest of his life to purging himself of his sin and constructing new meaning in his life. Ultimately, the meaning that Oedipus creates elevates him to tragic nobility. At the end of the story as Sophocles portrays it, Oedipus attains the status of a hero, purified and elevated by his years of suffering. So also are we free in this sense. We are free to construct meaning, even heroic

161

nobility, out of the most tragic situations. We are free, as Frankl put it, in the attitudes that we bring to the course of our destinies.

The ancient Stoics believed that freedom and happiness consisted in an attitude of detachment from the world. It is not, said the Stoic Epictetus, the things themselves that cause us unhappiness, but our opinions of things. Epictetus, who was the son of a slave and was for many years a slave himself, reflects that we are not in charge of our destinies. He tells us: "Remember you are an actor in a play, the character of which is determined by the playwright" (Epictetus, 1966, p.497).

The comparison of our lives to a play would seem to imply determinism rather than freedom and responsibility for our actions. It would seem to imply that the stories of our destinies are already written, and we merely perform what is in the script. But a play, since it is a construction of polysemic signs, gives itself over to a multitude of interpretations, a multitude of performances. Although a good director cannot change the text of the play, he can draw out a rich variety of meanings from the text. Each interpretation of a play, each performance, is as important dramatically as the text of the play itself. The text continues to evolve in each of its performances. The therapist is in this sense like the director of a play. He cannot change the events of a client's tragic past. But he can help the client draw out new meaning from the past, giving the text a new interpretation and the client a new direction for the future.

Ancient philosophers of ethics such as Epictetus struggled with the paradox of determinism and freedom just as we do today. The eighteenth century philosopher Kant, who was well-versed in Stoic ethics, made a very useful distinction. He said that we are capable of viewing other people as means towards our own ends (objects) or as ends-in-themselves (autonomous moral agents). If we view people as means, we merely *use* them. If we view people as ends-in-themselves we *respect* them. To act virtuously, argues Kant, we must view others as ends-in-themselves and not as means to our own selfish purposes. Kant went to great lengths to argue a fact that is clear to common sense, namely, that people are capable of acting from motives other than personal gain. What is not so evident to common sense is Kant's extension of this argument to say that action from unselfish motivation constitutes human happiness as well as human freedom.

For Kant, as for the Stoics, happiness consisted in the awareness of acting virtuously. Aristotle, similarly, defined happiness as activity in accordance with virtue. Clearly, this is not an especially prevalent definition of happiness in our own day, where peace of mind and nobility of character are not valued as highly as the ancients valued them. These values have been replaced in our society by the goal of accumulating material wealth. But Kant's idea that human beings may be viewed as either means or ends may still be instructive to us. It is, I would propose, the essence of ethics in therapy today, if not in all human relationships. All therapists know when they are putting their clients' best interests before their own or not. The beam of conscience may be bright, or it may be dimmed by many years of self-interest. But the light of conscience is there, whether or not it is followed. This notion, I believe, is similar to a thought that Jay Haley expressed when he wrote, some two decades ago:

> Practitioners who have done therapy for many years know what is ethical behavior and what is not. They may rationalize and attempt to deceive themselves and others about their own conduct, but they know. (1976, p.221)

The light by which we distinguish right action toward others from wrong action has been construed by various cultures at various periods of history in many different ways. The light may be thought of as internal, as the inner beam of conscience. Or the light may be thought to come from outside the individual person, in the form of society's precepts and laws. Or the source of illumination may be thought to transcend both the individual and society. But the light, reflected as in a mirror, is always there.

Bibliography

Aristotle. (1965). *The Poetics (W. Hamilton Fyfe, Trans.)*. Cambridge: Harvard.

Babcock, B. (Ed.). (1980a). Signs about signs: The Semiotics of self-reference [Special issue]. *Semiotica, 30* (1/2).

Babcock, B. (1980b). Reflexivity: Definitions and discriminations. *Semiotica, 30* (1/2), 1–14.

Bacon, F. (1955). *Selected writings of Francis Bacon (H. G. Dick, Ed.)*. New York: Modern Library. (Original work published 1620).

Bateson, G. (1972). *Steps to an ecology of mind*. New York: Ballantine.

Bateson, G. (1977). Play and paradigm. In G. Chick (Ed.), *Play & Culture 1* (1), 20–27.

Bateson, G. (1979). *Mind and nature: A necessary unity*. New York: Dutton.

Bateson, G., & Jackson, D. (1964). Some varieties of pathogenic organization. In D.Jackson (Ed.) *Communication, family, and marriage*. Palo Alto, CA: Science and Behavior.

Bateson, G., Jackson, D., Haley, J. & Weakland, J. (1956). Toward a theory of schizophrenia. In D.Jackson (Ed.) *Communication, family, and marriage*. Palo Alto, CA: Science and Behavior.

Bloch, D. (1978). *So the witch won't eat me: Fantasy and the child's fear of infanticide*. New York: Grove.

Burke, K. (1968). *Language as symbolic action*. Berkeley: University of California Press.

Burke, K. (1969). *A Grammar of Motives*. Berkeley: University of California Press.

Cassirer, E. (1957). *The philosophy of symbolic forms (R. Mannheim, Trans.)*. New Haven: Yale University Press.

Cassirer, E. (1970). *An essay on man*. New York: Bantam.

Dewey, J. (1916). *Essays in experimental logic*. New York: Dover.

Dewey, J. (1934). *Art as experience*. New York: Putnam.

Epictetus. (1966). The Encheiridion. In W. A. Oldfather (Ed. & Trans.), *The Discourses as reported by Arrian, The Manuel, and Fragments* (Vol.2). Cambridge: Harvard University Press.

Frankl, V. (1990). Video conversation hour at The Evolution of Psychotherapy conference, Las Vegas, Dec. 14, 1995.

Freud, S. (1900). The interpretation of dreams. In J. Strachey (Ed. & Trans.) *The Standard Edition of the Complete Psychological Works of Sigmund Freud* (vol. 4). New York: Norton.

Freud, S. (1905). Sexuality in the aetiology of the neuroses. In J. Strachey (Ed. & Trans.), *The Standard Edition of the Complete Psychological Works of Sigmund Freud*. New York: Norton.

Geertz, C. (1973). *The interpretation of cultures*. New York: Basic.

Geertz, C. (1986). Making experiences, authoring selves. In V. W. Turner & E. M. Bruner (Eds.), *The anthropology of experience*. Chicago: University of Illinois Press.

Gorfain, P. (1986). Play and the problem of knowing in *Hamlet*: An excursion into interpretive anthropology. In V. W. Turner and E. M. Bruner (Eds.), *The anthropology of experience*. Chicago: University of Illinois Press.

Haley, J. (1976). *Problem-solving therapy*. New York: Harper.

Haley, J. (1980). *Leaving home: The therapy of disturbed young people*. New York: McGraw-Hill.

Haley, J. (1984). *Ordeal therapy*. San Francisco: Jossey-Bass.

Haley, J. (1986). *Uncommon therapy*. New York: Norton.

Haley, J. (1990). *Strategies of psychotherapy*. Rockville, MD: Triangle.

Haley, J. (1993). *Jay Haley on Milton H. Erickson*. New York: Bruner/Mazel.

Hoffman, L. (1995). *The rise of social therapies*. Address presented at The Evolution of Psychotherapy conference, Las Vegas, December 16, 1995.

Huizinga, J. (1950). *Homo ludens: A study of the play-element in culture*. Boston: Beacon.

Jackson, D. (Ed.) (1968). *Communication, family and marriage*. Palo Alto, CA: Science and Behavior.

Kant, I. (1929). *Critique of pure reason (N. K. Smith, Trans.)*. New York: St. Martin's. (Original work published 1781).

Kuhn, T. (1970). *The structure of scientific revolutions*. Chicago: The University of Chicago Press.

Madanes, C. (1981). *Strategic family therapy*. San Francisco: Jossey-Bass.

Madanes, C. (1984). *Behind the one-way mirror*. San Francisco: Jossey-Bass.

Madanes, C. (1990). *Sex, love and violence*. New York: Norton.

Madanes, C. (1995). *The violence of men*. San Francisco: Jossey-Bass.

Mann, T. (1937). *Freud, Goethe, Wagner*. New York: Knopf.

Minuchin, S. (1974). *Families and family therapy*. Cambridge: Harvard University Press.

Minuchin, S. (1991). The seductions of constructivism. *Family Therapy Networker, 15*(5).

Minuchin, S. (1993). *Family healing: Tales of hope and renewal from family therapy*. New York: Free Press.

Montaigne, M. de. (1957). *The complete works of Montaigne (D. Frame, Trans.)*. Stanford: Stanford University Press. (Original work published 1580).

Peirce, C. S. (1955). The Fixation of belief. In J. Buchler (Ed.), *Philosophical writings of Peirce* (pp.5–22). New York: Dover. (Original work published 1877).

Peirce, C. S. (1955). How to make our ideas clear. In J. Buchler (Ed.), *Philosophical writings of Peirce* (pp.23-41). New York: Dover. (Original work published 1878).

Peirce, C. S. (1955). The scientific attitude and fallibilism. In J. Buchler (Ed.), *Philosophical writings of Peirce* (pp.42–59). New York: Dover. (Original work published 1896).

Peirce, C. S. (1955). Logic as Semiotic: The theory of signs. In J. Buchler (Ed.), *Philosophical writings of Peirce* (pp.98–119). New York: Dover. (Original work published 1897).

Peirce, C. S. (1955). Abduction and induction. In J. Buchler (Ed.), *Philosophical writings of Peirce* (pp.150-156). New York: Dover. (Original work published 1901).

Peirce, C. S. (1955). The essentials of Pragmatism. In J. Buchler (Ed.), *Philosophical Writings of Peirce*. New York: Dover. (Original work published in 1903).

Plato. (1969). *Republic*. Cambridge: Harvard University Press.

Plato. (1970). *Cratylus, Parmenides, Greater Hippias, Lesser Hippias*. Cambridge: Harvard University Press.

Schechner, R. (1988). Playing. In G. Chick (Ed.), *Play & Culture 1*(1) 3-27.

Sebeok, T. (1991). *A sign is just a sign*. Bloomington: Indiana University Press.

Simon, R. (1987). Good-bye paradox, hello invariant prescription: An interview with Mara Selvini Palazzoli. *Family Therapy Networker, 11,* 5.

Tolstoy, L. (1961). *Anna Karenina (D. Magerschack, Trans.).* New York: New American Library. (Original work published 1877).

Turner, V. (1967). *The forest of symbols.* Ithaca: Cornell University Press.

Turner, V. (1983). Body, brain and culture. *Zygon 18,* (3).

Turner, V. (1986). Experience and its expressions. In V. W. Turner & E. M. Bruner (Eds.), *The anthropology of experience.* Chicago: University of Illinois Press.

van Gennep, A. (1960). *The rites of passage.* Chicago: University of Chicago Press.

Varela, F. J. (1984). The creative circle: Sketches on the natural history of circularity. In P. Watzlawick (Ed.), *The invented reality* (pp.309–323). New York: Norton.

von Foerster, H. (1984). On constructing a reality. In P. Watzlawick (Ed.), *The invented reality* (pp.41–61). New York: Norton.

von Glasersfeld, E. (1984). An introduction to radical constructivism. In P. Watzlawick (Ed.), *The invented reality,* (pp.17–40). New York: Norton.

Watzlawick, P. (Ed.). (1984). *The invented reality.* New York: Norton.

Watzlawick, P. (1995, December 13). *To teach a different "game," or prescribing instead of interpreting.* Workshop presented at The Evolution of Psychotherapy conference, Las Vegas.

Wedge, M. (1994). Metaphorical reciprocity of symptoms. In M. Durrant (Ed.), *Case studies in brief and family therapy, 8* (1), 19–26.

White, M., & Epston, D. (1990). *Narrative means to therapeutic ends.* New York: Norton.

Whitehead, A. N., and Russell, B. (1910–1913). *Principia mathematica (Vols.1–3).* Cambridge: Cambridge University Press.

Winnicott, D. (1971). *Playing and reality.* London: Tavistock.

Index